THE CANDLE CAFE COOKBOOK

THE CANDLE CAFE COOKBOOK

MORE THAN 150 ENLIGHTENED RECIPES FROM NEW YORK'S RENOWNED VEGAN RESTAURANT

Joy Pierson and Bart Potenza
with Barbara Scott-Goodman

CLARKSON POTTER/PUBLISHERS
NEW YORK

Published by Clarkson Potter/Publishers, New York, New York.
Member of the Crown Publishing Group, a division of Random House, Inc.
www.randomhouse.com

CLARKSON N. POTTER is a trademark and POTTER and colophon are registered trademarks
of Random House, Inc.

Printed in the United States of America

Design by Jan Derevjanik

Library of Congress Cataloging-in-Publication Data
Pierson, Joy.
    The Candle Cafe cookbook : more than 150 enlightened recipes from New York's renowned
vegan restaurant / Joy Pierson and Bart Potenza with Barbara Scott-Goodman.—1st ed.
1. Vegan cookery. I. Potenza, Bart. II. Scott-Goodman, Barbara. III. Title.
    TX837 .P5293 2003
641.5'636—dc21   2002153324

ISBN 0-609-80981-4

10 9 8 7

First Edition

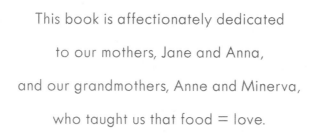

This book is affectionately dedicated

to our mothers, Jane and Anna,

and our grandmothers, Anne and Minerva,

who taught us that food = love.

ACKNOWLEDGMENTS

The Candle Cafe Cookbook involved the hard work and support of many people whom we'd like to thank.

We are grateful to our talented chefs, who gave us their inspiring recipes: Jorge Pineda, Angel Ramos, Valentino Dominguez, Theresa Preston, Abigael Birrell, Mark Felix, Chris Fox, Cliff Preefer, Jonathan Grumbles, and Paul Rabin. Thank you to our managers, who take good care of our restaurant and customers: Mourad Menber, Germaine Albert, and Trina Fosness. We'd also like to thank our waitstaff, bartenders, barbacks, phone expeditors, runners, and dishwashers, who keep the restaurant running smoothly, and Eric Adjei, who makes sure all the bills get paid.

For testing and retesting the recipes, we are grateful to Stephanie Zinowski for her hard work and dedication, to David Baden for his enthusiasm and lightness of being, to the Sirkins and Baby Alec for tasting our recipes with open hearts and minds, and to Beth and David Tunick for the use of their lovely home and kitchen.

We are deeply appreciative of the organic farmers who grow only the best and deliver the goods to us daily: Guy Jones, Lisa and Mark Dunau, Steve Sanger, and Joshua Steinhauser, who digs ever so deeply for the best. The devotion and support of PETA, Farm Sanctuary, Earthsave, PCRM, and Co-op America have played a significant role in our success as a vegan restaurant.

Heartfelt thanks go to our many good friends who have supported us along the way: to Benay Vynerib, whose commitment to the Candle Cafe and the vegan movement inspires us all; Linda Nealon and Mary Max, who keep us on our vegan toes; and Alicia, Woody, and Laura, whose love and encouragement has kept us going. Thanks also to Renée Loux Underkoffler and Andrea Beaman, who continue to share their creative cooking talents and nutritional knowledge with us, and Jessica Greenfield, for her loyalty and for being a living example of the beauty of veganism. A special thanks to Madeline Green, who works with us to educate and nourish the children of Harlem.

Love and thanks to our families, including Vaj Potenza, for his hands-on help and great sense of humor; to all the Felensteins and the Kerners, including Grant, Laura, Jamie, and Melissa, who are among our many nieces and nephews and are an inspiration for us to make the world a better place for future generations. Thanks also to our families and friends who continue to confirm that vegan food from our recipes tastes great.

We are very grateful to Margot Schupf, who encouraged us to write this book and began the project; our agent, Andrew Blauner, who worked closely with us from beginning to end; and our in-house editing staff, Michelle Sumners, Veronica Ortiz, and Temple Brooks. Many thanks to the people at Clarkson Potter: Pam Krauss, Adina Steiman, our editor, for her insight, support, and patience; Marysarah Quinn and Jan Derevjanik for their design talents; and Jean Lynch and Linnea Knollmueller for smoothing the path through production. Thanks also go to Michael Grimm, for his beautiful photography, Roscoe Betsill for his impeccable food styling, and to our co-author, Barbara Scott-Goodman, who brought us a wealth of cookbook knowledge in both her writing and her art direction of the superb photographs inside this book and gracing the cover.

Finally, we thank our thousands of customers and friends, who really inspired us to write this cookbook in the first place—and anyone who has ever eaten a vegetable—and that's all of us, isn't it?

CONTENTS

THE CANDLE CAFE COOKBOOK

INTRODUCTION: THE STORY OF THE CANDLE CAFE

The Candle Cafe originated in the summer of 1984 when Bart purchased Sunny's, a landmark health food store and juice bar located on Manhattan's Upper East Side. Many rich and famous denizens of the neighborhood, such as Anne Lindbergh and Mrs. Thomas Dewey, frequented Sunny's for their daily carrot juices. Legend has it that the owners, two rather eccentric women, lit candles all over the store every evening to bless their establishment. Naturally their neighbors objected to this sacred ritual (and fire hazard), so it came to an end. But Bart was so taken with their tradition that he renamed the restaurant Healthy Candle when he purchased it.

In 1987, Joy began frequenting Healthy Candle as a customer, health counselor, and friend. She eventually became the in-house nutritionist for the fast-growing eatery. Bart was so impressed by her commitment to the vegetarian and holistic movement that he made her a partner in the business. Their belief that they could make a difference in people's lives by feeding them fresh and wholesome food led them to explore the possibility of expanding.

The philospher Goethe once said, ". . . the moment one definitely commits oneself, then Providence moves too." So Joy and Bart committed and began the search for a good location for their new restaurant. After two years of looking, they finally found the right space, a vacant restaurant at 1307 Third Avenue. They called the landlord and began negotiations in a "New York minute." Although the costs of renovating, outfitting, and decorating a restaurant were much steeper than they had imagined, they remained committed to their dream.

A LUCKY DAY

On a very hot August 13, 1993, Friday the thirteenth no less, Bart and Joy bought a lottery ticket in the New York State Take Five game. They played a combination of their birthday numbers, as they often did, and they got lucky. They won $53,000 and were on their way. After raising a bit more from their families, friends, and loyal customers, they had the seed money for their new restaurant, the Candle Cafe.

Now in its ninth year, the Candle Cafe has garnered a major following committed to what Bart and Joy created. The restaurant is a huge success and has been praised and acknowledged as New York's best vegetarian restaurant by both the holistic and traditional communities.

COOKING AT THE CANDLE

Through the years we've encouraged the talent and creativity of our chefs and cooks. There is an apprenticeship that goes along with good vegan cooking, and our chefs have openly shared their gifts and secrets with each other, and now with you through this cookbook.

Our attempt at creating the best possible vegan cookbook for you has been very challenging, because many of our gifted chefs have unique and sometimes unconventional approaches to the food they create. Recording their often esoteric cooking styles required us to spend endless hours checking and cross-checking recipes so that they would be easy and understandable for you, the home cook.

We believe that everyone has a personal chef within him- or herself. We invite you to think of yourself as part of our team as you begin to prepare these delicious recipes using what we share with you as a guideline. Feel free to call on your inner cook and add your own special touches and variations to each recipe.

Vegan food, enhanced by organic ingredients, has become a necessity for the planet and the health and well-being of the individuals who occupy it. Fortunately for many, they are being fed and comforted by the vegan foods prepared at the Candle Cafe. Now, we invite you to take these delicious and inspiring recipes into your own home and the homes of your friends and loved ones.

APPETIZERS

Appetizers entice guests to the table to share and enjoy food. Whether served as a sit-down first course, on buffet-style platters, or as small bites or tapas from passed-around trays, they always say welcome, especially when served with wine or cocktails. At the Candle, we've developed an array of unique and delicious appetizers—from elegant Grilled Vegetable Napoleons and savory mezze and crostini platters to simple spreads, dips, and salsas served with crudités, homemade toasts, and chips. Keep a bowlful of Babaganoush in your refrigerator to snack on, or cook up a quesadilla for a light meal. This chapter is chock-full of recipes suitable for all occasions and appetites.

TOBELLO AND RED PEPPER QUESADILLAS

serves 4

...se quesadillas are perfect for a party. You can serve them as an appetizer, or cut them into smaller wedges for the perfect portable finger food. They're also great when you want a light bite along with soup or salad. The bean purée can be prepared well ahead of time and works with almost any kind of bean.

BEAN PURÉE

- 1 CUP WHITE, BLACK, OR PINTO BEANS
- 1 1-INCH PIECE OF KOMBU
- 1 MINCED GARLIC CLOVE, OR ½ TEASPOON GARLIC POWDER
- ½ TEASPOON CHILI OR CHIPOTLE POWDER
- ½ TEASPOON SEA SALT
- 1 TEASPOON FRESH LIME JUICE
- 2 TABLESPOONS CHOPPED CILANTRO

QUESADILLA FILLING

- 2 LARGE PORTOBELLO MUSHROOMS, THINLY SLICED
- 1 RED BELL PEPPER, STEMMED, SEEDED, AND THINLY SLICED
- 1 TABLESPOON EXTRA-VIRGIN OLIVE OIL SEA SALT FRESHLY GROUND BLACK PEPPER

- 2 12-INCH FLOUR TORTILLAS
- 1 SMALL RED ONION, VERY THINLY SLICED
- ⅔ CUP GRATED SOY CHEESE

1. First, prepare the bean purée. Pick over and rinse the beans and put them in a bowl with the piece of kombu, add enough water to cover by about 2 inches, and set aside to soak for 6 to 8 hours or overnight.

2. Drain the beans, reserving the kombu, and transfer them both to a soup pot. Add 6 cups of water and bring to a boil over high heat. Reduce the heat and simmer the beans, uncovered, for 40 to 50 minutes, until just tender. Drain and set aside, reserving about a cup of cooking liquid.

3. Transfer the beans to a food processor or blender. Add the garlic, chili powder, sea salt, lime juice, cilantro, and a bit of the cooking liquid and pulse until smooth. Taste and adjust the seasonings. The purée can be made up to 3 days ahead of time and kept in the refrigerator.

4. Preheat the oven to 350°F.

5. Prepare the quesadilla filling: Toss the mushrooms and pepper in olive oil and salt and pepper to taste. Place on a baking sheet in a single layer and roast for 30 to 45 minutes. Set aside.

6. Assemble the quesadillas: Spread a thin layer of the bean purée onto a tortilla. Top with half the roasted mushroom-pepper mixture and half the onion slices. Sprinkle half the cheese over the vegetables and repeat with the second tortilla. Fold the tortillas in half.

7. Bake the quesadillas until warmed through, about 15 minutes, turning once. Or, for a crisper result, broil or grill the quesadillas for about 5 minutes per side. Cut into quarters and serve at once.

WATER

We use filtered or purified water in all of our restaurant cooking. We recognize that this type of water is not always available or practical for the home cook, but do try to use it if possible.

PIZZADILLAS

serves 4 to 6

Inspired by his Italian roots, Bart created the pizzadilla, a great variation on the quesadilla. It's loads of fun to make and always a big hit with kids. Use your favorite bottled organic tomato sauce or our homemade Marinara Sauce.

- 2 GARLIC CLOVES, PEELED
- 1 TABLESPOON EXTRA-VIRGIN OLIVE OIL
- 1 CUP MARINARA SAUCE (SEE PAGE 163)
- 2 12-INCH FLOUR TORTILLAS
- 1 CUP GRATED SOY CHEESE
- ½ CUP FINELY CHOPPED FRESH BASIL

- 8 SUN-DRIED TOMATOES, SOAKED IN HOT WATER FOR 10 MINUTES, DRAINED, AND THINLY SLICED
- SEA SALT
- ½ TEASPOON DRIED OREGANO
- ½ TEASPOON CRUSHED RED PEPPER FLAKES (OPTIONAL)

1. Preheat the oven to 350°F.

2. Place the garlic cloves in a small baking pan and drizzle with the olive oil. Bake until softened, 10 to 15 minutes. When cool enough to handle, cut into thin slices.

3. Spread a layer of marinara sauce on each tortilla. Top with the soy cheese, basil, roasted garlic, and sun-dried tomatoes. Sprinkle with salt to taste, oregano, and red pepper flakes, if using. Fold each tortilla in half and bake for 10 minutes, or until warmed through.

4. Cut the tortillas into quarters and serve at once.

EQUIPMENT

Most of our recipes do not require equipment that would not be found in any well-outfitted kitchen. In many of our recipes we use a blender or a food processor to blend or purée appetizer dips and spreads, soups, salad dressings, sauces, and some desserts. Also, because we use so many chopped fruits and vegetables in our food, we highly recommend using top-quality, well-sharpened kitchen knives.

GRILLED VEGETABLE NAPOLEON

serves 6

We serve this bona fide restaurant favorite as an appetizer on Valentine's Day.
It's also perfect to start off dinner parties for friends.

VEGETABLES

- 2 MEDIUM EGGPLANTS, SLICED
  SEA SALT
- 2 TABLESPOONS EXTRA-VIRGIN
  OLIVE OIL
- 1 TEASPOON BALSAMIC VINEGAR
- 2 GARLIC CLOVES, MINCED
- ½ TEASPOON DRIED BASIL
- ½ TEASPOON DRIED OREGANO
- ½ TEASPOON CRUSHED RED PEPPER
  FLAKES
- 1 LARGE ZUCCHINI, SLICED
- 1 RED ONION, PEELED AND SLICED

RED PEPPER COULIS

- 2 RED PEPPERS
- 1 GARLIC CLOVE, MINCED
- ½ TEASPOON SEA SALT
- 1 TEASPOON CHOPPED FRESH
  ROSEMARY
- 1 TEASPOON EXTRA-VIRGIN OLIVE OIL

- 1 POUND PACKAGED POLENTA
  (WE LIKE NATE'S ORGANIC BRAND)
  FRESH PARSLEY, FOR GARNISH

1. Place the eggplant slices in a colander and sprinkle a generous amount of sea salt over them. Let stand for 20 minutes. Drain the eggplant and pat dry with paper towels. In a large bowl, mix the olive oil, vinegar, garlic, basil, oregano, and red pepper flakes together. Add the eggplant, zucchini, and onion slices, toss to coat, and let stand for 1 hour.

2. For the red pepper coulis, place the peppers on the open flame of a gas burner or on a baking sheet under a broiler until the skin is blackened. Cover the peppers with paper towels. Let stand 10 minutes, then use the paper towels to wipe off the burnt skin. Remove the stem and seeds and chop coarsely. Transfer the peppers to a blender, add ½ cup of water, the garlic, salt, rosemary, and olive oil, and blend until smooth.

3. Meanwhile, prepare the polenta or corn grits according to package directions. Cut into rounds, set aside, and keep warm.

4. On an oiled grill over medium heat, or under the broiler on a baking tray, cook the eggplant, zucchini, and onion until softened, about 10 minutes per side.

5. To assemble each napoleon, spoon a bit of red pepper coulis onto a plate, top with an eggplant slice, a polenta round, a zucchini slice, and an onion slice. Garnish each napoleon with fresh parsley and serve at once.

MINI POTATO LATKES

makes 3 dozen mini pancakes, serves 6 to 8

You can still enjoy potato latkes with our lightened-up recipe, which uses applesauce or flax eggs instead of eggs. Served with tofu sour cream and homemade applesauce, or with a touch of hiziki caviar (opposite page), these potato pancakes are always a hit at our parties.

- 4 TO 6 LARGE RUSSET POTATOES, PEELED
- 2 MEDIUM ONIONS, PEELED AND QUARTERED
- 4 TABLESPOONS APPLESAUCE OR 2 TABLESPOONS FLAX EGGS (SEE BELOW)
- ¼ CUP FLOUR OR MATZO MEAL

- PINCH OF BAKING POWDER
- SEA SALT
- FRESHLY GROUND BLACK PEPPER
- ¼ CUP SAFFLOWER OIL (OPTIONAL), PLUS MORE FOR FRYING
- HOMEMADE APPLESAUCE (PAGE 170)
- TOFU-CILANTRO SOUR CREAM (PAGE 167)

1. Put the potatoes and onions in a large bowl filled with cold water to prevent discoloring. Grate half of the potatoes in a food processor, then grate half the onions, the remaining half of the potatoes, and then the remaining half of the onions. Drain the potato and onion mixture in a colander. When drained, put back in the food processor with the metal blade attachment and pulse again a few times. The mixture should be a bit coarse. (You can also grate the potatoes and onions by hand, but that's a lot more work!) Drain again, then put in a large bowl.

2. Stir in the applesauce or flax eggs, flour or matzo meal, ¼ cup oil if using, baking powder, and salt and pepper to taste.

3. Heat the oil, if using, in a large skillet, or heat a large nonstick skillet and drop heaping tablespoons of the potato mixture into it. When the edges begin to brown, turn the pancakes over and cook until golden brown, about 3 minutes per side. Drain on paper towels and repeat with the remaining potato-onion mixture.

4. Serve the pancakes hot, with applesauce and sour cream on the side.

FLAX EGGS

We substitute flax eggs, made from flax seeds and water, for fresh dairy eggs in many of our recipes. To make them, place 2 parts warm water in a blender container and add 1 part flax seeds. Let sit for 15 minutes, then blend at high speed until they are gelatinous and the flax seeds are no longer visible. The remaining flax eggs will keep, covered, in the refrigerator for up to 2 weeks.

EGGPLANT-HIZIKI CAVIAR

serves 6 to 8

We love to serve this "caviar" in many ways for a festive party appetizer.
It's excellent served with Tofu-Cilantro Sour Cream (page 167) on small
roasted potatoes or as a topping for Mini Potato Latkes (opposite), garnished
with fresh parsley and red peppers. We also like it spread on Crostini (page 26)
and Oven-Baked Pita Crisps (page 17).

---

1 CUP HIZIKI

1 MEDIUM EGGPLANT, HALVED
LENGTHWISE

2 TABLESPOONS SESAME OIL
SEA SALT

2 LARGE SHALLOTS, PEELED AND
FINELY MINCED

1 GARLIC CLOVE, PEELED AND MINCED

2 TABLESPOONS AGAVE NECTAR

2 TABLESPOONS BROWN RICE VINEGAR

1. Preheat the oven to 425°F.

2. Soak the hiziki in hot water for 30 minutes. Drain and set aside.

3. Rub the eggplant halves with 1 tablespoon of the sesame oil and sprinkle with sea salt.
Place them on a baking sheet and bake for 20 minutes, until soft inside. Remove from the
oven and set aside to cool. Scoop out the flesh and place in a large bowl.

4. In a sauté pan, heat the remaining tablespoon of sesame oil over medium heat. Add the
shallots and garlic and cook for about 1 minute. Add the drained hiziki and cook an additional 5 minutes. Add enough water just to cover the mixture and stir in 1 tablespoon each
agave nectar and brown rice vinegar. Simmer, uncovered, until the liquid evaporates.
Remove from the heat and cool. Chop finely and add to the cooked eggplant. Stir in the
remaining agave nectar and vinegar.

5. Chill the caviar for at least 2 hours or up to overnight before serving.

 VARIATION: To serve hiziki as a garnish that closely resembles caviar, omit the eggplant and finely chop the hiziki mixture. Sprinkle over latkes, toast points, or small roasted
potato halves for appetizers, or use as a garnish for many dishes.

SOAKING SEA VEGETABLE

We often use dried seaweed in our recipes. To reconstitute sea vegetable, soak in boiling
water to cover for about 10 minutes. Drain, rinse, and add cold water to cover for about
10 minutes. Drain again.

GEFILTE TOFU

makes 24 pieces, serves 6 to 8

We like to make Gefilte Tofu for the holidays. It can be easily prepared ahead of time, and the flavors are actually enhanced by overnight chilling. Joy's grandma, whose own mother made her gefilte fish from scratch, loved this version, much to her granddaughter's delight.

---

1 TABLESPOON SAFFLOWER OIL

1 LARGE ONION, PEELED AND FINELY DICED

2 GARLIC CLOVES, MINCED

1 CELERY STALK, FINELY DICED

PINCH OF SEA SALT

PINCH OF FRESHLY GROUND BLACK PEPPER

2 CARROTS, PEELED AND GRATED

1 POUND FIRM TOFU, DRAINED AND CRUMBLED

1 POUND SOFT TOFU, DRAINED AND MASHED

½ CUP MATZO MEAL

1 TEASPOON AGAR POWDER

1 ½ TEASPOONS ARROWROOT POWDER

PREPARED HORSERADISH, FOR GARNISH

1. In a skillet, heat the oil and add the onion, garlic, celery, salt and pepper. Cook over medium heat for 4 minutes, stirring. Add the carrots and cook for an additional 2 minutes. Remove from the heat and set aside to cool.

2. In a large bowl, mix together both types of tofu, the matzo meal, and agar and arrowroot powders, then stir in the vegetables. Let the mixture stand for 1 hour.

3. Form into 1- by 2-inch patties. Steam them in a vegetable steamer over medium heat for 15 minutes. Remove them with a slotted spoon and chill for 3 hours or up to overnight.

4. Serve chilled with a dollop of horseradish on each patty.

VARIATION: To make a delicious salad that resembles chopped egg salad, crumble leftover Gefilte Tofu and add Vegan Mayo (page 166), chopped celery, and fresh herbs.

PHYLLO TRIANGLES

makes 30 triangles, serves 6 to 8

Phyllo triangles are wonderful hors d'oeuvres. We make them often for cocktail parties, picnics, and other events. Our version of the classic spinach pie triangles is a delicious one, filled with fresh spinach, herbs, and tofu. They can be made well ahead of time and frozen. To reheat, just bake at 350°F for 25 to 30 minutes, or until warmed through.

FILLING

2 TABLESPOONS EXTRA-VIRGIN OLIVE OIL

2 BUNCHES OF FRESH OR 2 10-OUNCE PACKAGES ORGANIC FROZEN SPINACH, RINSED AND COARSELY CHOPPED

1 SMALL ONION, FINELY DICED

2 GARLIC CLOVES, MINCED

2 TEASPOONS SEA SALT

FRESHLY GROUND BLACK PEPPER

2 TABLESPOONS FINELY CHOPPED FRESH DILL

2 TABLESPOONS FINELY CHOPPED FRESH BASIL

1 POUND EXTRA-FIRM TOFU, MASHED

1 TABLESPOON WHITE MISO

1 TEASPOON NUTRITIONAL YEAST

1 PACKAGE PHYLLO DOUGH SHEETS (ABOUT 15 SHEETS), THAWED (SEE NOTE)

EXTRA-VIRGIN OLIVE OIL OR OLIVE OIL SPRAY

1. In a skillet, heat 1 tablespoon of the olive oil. Add the spinach and sauté until wilted. Drain well and set aside.

2. Heat the remaining oil in the same pan and add the onion, garlic, salt, and pepper to taste and cook over medium heat for 5 minutes. Remove from the heat, stir in the dill and basil, and set aside.

3. Combine the spinach and onion mixtures together, then stir in the tofu, miso, and yeast. Refrigerate until ready to assemble.

4. Spray or brush a phyllo sheet with olive oil. Top with 2 more sheets, spraying or brushing with olive oil between each one. Cut the layered sheets lengthwise into 5 equal strips.

5. Place 2 teaspoons of filling in the corner of the strip. Fold one corner over to cover the filling. Fold the newly created point down. Repeat until you come to the last fold, making sure that the bottom is well oiled so that the flap sticks to the triangle. Brush or spray with olive oil.

6. Preheat the oven to 350°F, and bake for 15 to 18 minutes, until lightly browned.

NOTE: Whole wheat or spelt flour phyllo dough, available in health food stores, can also be used. A good brand is The Fillo Factory.

CANDLE CAFE'S MEZZE PLATTER

Our restaurant is renowned for its mezze platter, which has been on the menu for many years. This combination of healthy Middle Eastern dishes is just right for serving as an appetizer or at a big party along with Oven-Baked Pita Crisps (page 17), crudités, and bowls of black olives.

To assemble the mezze platter (on individual plates or one large serving platter), spread Hummus on the plate or platter. Make a well in the center with the back of a spoon, fill with Tabouli, and top with Babaganoush. Garnish with black olives and lemon slices.

HUMMUS

makes 2 cups, enough for 1 large or 6 individual mezze platters

We like to make Hummus with dried chickpeas, though if you're short on time use canned ones.

2 CUPS COOKED CHICKPEAS (PAGE 211), COOKING LIQUID RESERVED, OR 2 CUPS DRAINED CANNED CHICKPEAS, LIQUID RESERVED

2 LARGE GARLIC CLOVES, MINCED

¼ CUP FRESH LEMON JUICE

¼ TEASPOON CAYENNE

½ TEASPOON PAPRIKA

½ TEASPOON GROUND CUMIN

½ TEASPOON SEA SALT

½ CUP CHOPPED PARSLEY

⅓ CUP EXTRA-VIRGIN OLIVE OIL, PLUS MORE FOR GARNISH

⅔ CUP SESAME TAHINI

LEMON SLICES, GREEK OLIVES, AND MINT OR PARSLEY SPRIGS, FOR GARNISH

1. In a large bowl, combine all of the ingredients except the garnishes and stir to mix well. Place in a food processor fitted with the steel blade and process briefly. Add ½ cup of water or the chickpea cooking liquid and continue to blend until the mixture is smooth and almost fluffy. Add more of the liquid if necessary to loosen the mixture. Scrape down the sides of the bowl once or twice. Transfer to a serving bowl and refrigerate for at least 1 hour. (The Hummus can be made up to 3 days ahead and refrigerated. Return to room temperature before serving.)

2. To serve on its own, drizzle a bit of olive oil over the Hummus and sprinkle a bit of paprika. Garnish with lemon slices, olives, and mint or parsley sprigs.

VARIATIONS: Hummus can also be made with black or white beans.

BABAGANOUSH

makes about 4 cups, enough for 1 large or 6 individual mezze platters

When making Babaganoush, be careful not to make it too smooth in the
food processor. It should retain a fairly chunky texture.

4 SMALL EGGPLANTS

1 TABLESPOON EXTRA-VIRGIN OLIVE OIL

1 LARGE GARLIC CLOVE, MINCED

½ CUP SESAME TAHINI

½ CUP VEGAN MAYO (PAGE 166)

½ TEASPOON SEA SALT

1 TEASPOON FRESHLY GROUND BLACK PEPPER

1. Preheat the oven to 425°F.

2. Cut the eggplants in half lengthwise and score the flesh with a small knife. Place cut-side down on a lightly oiled baking sheet and bake until the eggplants are very soft, about 30 to 40 minutes.

3. When the eggplants are cool enough to handle, place the halves flesh side up and, using a small spoon, scrape out and discard as many of the bitter seeds as possible. Scoop out the rest of the flesh into the bowl of a food processor fitted with the steel blade.

4. Add the olive oil, garlic, tahini, Vegan Mayo, salt, and pepper and process, being careful not to make the mixture too smooth. Taste and adjust the seasonings, if necessary. The Babaganoush can be refrigerated for up to 3 days. Bring to room temperature before serving.

5. Transfer to a bowl and serve with pita crisps or flatbread.

TABOULI

makes about 3 cups, enough for 1 large or 6 individual mezze platters

Although tabouli is traditionally made with bulgur or cracked wheat, we often make it with couscous or quinoa. Use whichever you prefer—any way, it's delicious.

½ CUP UNCOOKED COUSCOUS, BULGUR, OR QUINOA (SEE NOTE)

4 TABLESPOONS EXTRA-VIRGIN OLIVE OIL

½ CUP BOILING WATER

2 MEDIUM TOMATOES, DICED

1 SMALL RED ONION, PEELED AND DICED

2 GARLIC CLOVES, MINCED

1 LARGE BUNCH OF PARSLEY, COARSELY CHOPPED

½ BUNCH OF MINT, COARSELY CHOPPED

2 TABLESPOONS FRESH LEMON JUICE

SEA SALT

FRESHLY GROUND BLACK PEPPER

1. Put the couscous in a large bowl. Add the olive oil and boiling water and mix well. Cover the bowl with plastic wrap and let sit until the water is absorbed into the grains, about 20 minutes. Uncover and let cool. The grains should have swelled to about 2 cups.

2. In a medium bowl, mix together the tomatoes, onion, garlic, parsley, mint, and lemon juice, then add to the grain mixture. Add salt and pepper to taste. Serve cool or at room temperature.

NOTE: If using quinoa, rinse with cold water until the water runs clear and drain before cooking. If using bulgur or quinoa, follow the cooking instructions on page 210.

OVEN-BAKED PITA CRISPS

makes about 36 crisps, serves 6

We make pita crisps for all types of dips and spreads as well as for soups.
They are an excellent accompaniment to our Mezze Platter and can be made
ahead of time. They keep very well when stored in an airtight container.

1 TABLESPOON FINELY GROUND
FENNEL SEEDS (OPTIONAL;
SEE NOTE)

1 TEASPOON GARLIC POWDER

½ TEASPOON PAPRIKA

PINCH OF CAYENNE

PINCH OF SEA SALT

2 TABLESPOONS EXTRA-VIRGIN
OLIVE OIL

3 PITA POCKETS, SPLIT HORIZONTALLY
AND CUT INTO 2-INCH WEDGES

1. Preheat the oven to 350°F.

2. In a small bowl, mix together the fennel seeds, garlic powder, paprika, cayenne, and salt.
Whisk in the olive oil.

3. Put the spice and oil mixture and the pita pieces in a large bowl. Toss together thoroughly.
Drizzle with a bit of extra olive oil if the pita wedges seem too dry. Place on a baking
sheet and bake until crisp, about 20 minutes.

NOTE: You can use a mortar and pestle or a coffee grinder to grind the fennel seeds.

TOFU SATAY WITH COCONUT-PEANUT SAUCE

makes 16 skewers, serves 6 to 8

Satays, grilled or broiled skewers from Southeast Asia, are addictively good appetizer and cocktail party fare. Our version includes the refreshing counterpoint of pear tomatoes and cucumbers. Served with spicy Coconut-Peanut Sauce, it's always a winner.

---

2 TABLESPOONS BROWN RICE VINEGAR

2 TABLESPOONS UMEBOSHI VINEGAR

½ TEASPOON CRUSHED RED PEPPER FLAKES

1 TABLESPOON GRATED FRESH GINGER

¼ CUP SHOYU OR TAMARI SOY SAUCE

1 TABLESPOON CHOPPED CILANTRO

1 TABLESPOON CHOPPED FRESH MINT

1 GARLIC CLOVE, MINCED

1 POUND FIRM TOFU, CUT INTO 16 CUBES

1 LARGE CUCUMBER, PEELED, SEEDED, AND CUT INTO 16 PIECES

16 YELLOW OR RED PEAR TOMATOES

COCONUT-PEANUT SAUCE (RECIPE FOLLOWS)

1. Place the vinegars, red pepper flakes, ginger, shoyu or tamari soy sauce, cilantro, mint, garlic, and 2 tablespoons water in a blender and blend until smooth. Toss the mixture with the tofu cubes and let marinate for at least an hour or as long as overnight.

2. Preheat the oven to 375°F.

3. Spread the tofu in a single layer on a baking sheet and bake for 25 minutes, turning once or twice, until nicely browned. Remove the tofu from the oven and set aside to cool.

4. To assemble the satay, place a cube of tofu on a small bamboo or metal skewer, top with a cucumber piece, then a tomato. Serve with the Coconut-Peanut Sauce.

COCONUT-PEANUT SAUCE

makes 2½ cups

½ CUP PEANUT BUTTER

½ CUP COCONUT MILK

¼ CUP BROWN RICE VINEGAR

1 THAI BIRD CHILI OR 1 JALAPEÑO, SEEDED (SEE NOTE)

½ CUP SHOYU OR TAMARI SOY SAUCE

2 TABLESPOONS CHOPPED CILANTRO

2 TABLESPOONS CHOPPED FRESH MINT

1 TABLESPOON GRATED FRESH GINGER

1 GARLIC CLOVE, MINCED

Place all of the ingredients with ¼ cup water in a blender and blend until smooth. The sauce will keep, covered, in the refrigerator for up to 7 days. Serve at room temperature.

NOTE: Thai bird chilies are fiery-hot dried chilies used extensively in Szechuan and Thai cuisines. They are packaged and sold in health food stores and gourmet and Asian markets. If you prefer less heat in your sauce, substitute jalapeños.

SEITAN SKEWERS WITH CHIMICHURRI CITRUS-HERB SAUCE

makes about 12 skewers, serves 6

Here is one of the restaurant's all-time favorites. We have been known to ship these appetizers to friends and customers on the West Coast who have called in need of a fix. These seitan skewers are wonderful when well charred and served with refreshing Chimichurri Citrus-Herb Sauce. They freeze very well and are great to have on hand to serve as appetizers, snacks, or an entrée.

MARINADE

- 1 CUP FRESH LEMON JUICE
- 1 CUP EXTRA-VIRGIN OLIVE OIL
- 2 GARLIC CLOVES, MINCED
- ¼ CUP AGAVE NECTAR
- 1 TEASPOON SEA SALT
- ½ CUP FINELY CHOPPED PARSLEY
- 1 CUP FINELY CHOPPED CILANTRO

1½ POUNDS SEITAN, CUT INTO 1½-INCH PIECES

CHIMICHURRI CITRUS-HERB SAUCE

- 1 CUP FRESH ORANGE JUICE
- ¼ CUP FRESH LEMON JUICE
- ¼ CUP FRESH LIME JUICE
- 1 CUP EXTRA-VIRGIN OLIVE OIL
- ¼ CUP SILKEN TOFU
- ¼ CUP CHOPPED PARSLEY
- 2 TABLESPOONS AGAVE NECTAR

SEA SALT

1. To prepare the marinade, put all of the marinade ingredients in a blender. Blend on high speed until well combined.

2. Put 4 pieces of seitan on each of 12 metal or bamboo skewers. Place them in a large non-reactive bowl or baking dish, pour the marinade over them, and let marinate for at least 1 hour or up to overnight.

3. To prepare the Chimichurri Citrus-Herb Sauce, put all of the chimichurri ingredients in a blender. Blend on high speed until well combined. Refrigerate until ready to use.

4. Prepare a charcoal, gas, or stove-top grill. Grill the skewers over medium-high heat until well browned, about 5 to 7 minutes per side. Serve immediately, drizzled with the Chimichurri Citrus-Herb Sauce.

SAVORY STUFFED MUSHROOMS

serves 6

Fresh spinach and chopped walnuts make a light and lovely filling for whole mushrooms. Whether served on trays at a cocktail party or over mixed salad greens drizzled with a bit of olive oil, they are wonderful.

2 TABLESPOONS EXTRA-VIRGIN OLIVE OIL

1 GARLIC CLOVE, MINCED

⅓ CUP FINELY CHOPPED ONIONS

1 POUND MUSHROOMS, FINELY CHOPPED

PINCH OF DRIED BASIL

PINCH OF DRIED THYME

1 CUP CHOPPED WALNUTS

1 CUP COOKED SPINACH, WELL DRAINED AND FINELY CHOPPED

PINCH OF SEA SALT

FRESHLY GROUND BLACK PEPPER

¼ CUP WHOLE WHEAT BREAD CRUMBS (SEE NOTE)

16–24 LARGE BUTTON MUSHROOMS, STEMMED AND LEFT WHOLE

1. Preheat the oven to 350°F.

2. Heat the oil in a large skillet over medium-high heat and sauté the garlic, onions, and mushrooms for 10 minutes. Add the basil, thyme, walnuts, spinach, and salt and pepper to taste and mix very well. Remove from the heat and stir in the bread crumbs.

3. Stuff each mushroom with the filling and place on a baking sheet. Bake for 6 to 8 minutes and serve warm.

NOTE: To make whole wheat bread crumbs, trim the crusts from 2 slices of day-old whole wheat bread and pulverize in the food processor. In a pinch, commercial unflavored bread crumbs can also be used, but check the ingredients—most contain dairy.

CRYSTAL ROLLS

makes 4 rolls, serves 4

These crystal rolls make an elegant and incredibly tasty hors d'oeuvre to enjoy
with wine or mixed drinks. It's best to have all the ingredients ready before rolling
them into rice paper wrappers so that they don't dry out. For a larger gathering,
simply double or triple the recipe and serve them on platters with
Spicy Thai Dipping Sauce (page 161) or B-12 Tamari Dijon (page 164).

- 4 OUNCES THIN RICE NOODLES
- 4 12-INCH-DIAMETER RICE PAPER WRAPPERS (SEE NOTE)
- 1 BLOCK MARINATED GRILLED TOFU (PAGE 153), CUT INTO ½-INCH STRIPS
- ½ CUP CHOPPED PEANUTS
- 1 RED BELL PEPPER, SEEDED AND JULIENNED, THEN CUT INTO 1-INCH LENGTHS

- 1 SMALL CUCUMBER, PEELED, SEEDED, AND JULIENNED, THEN CUT INTO 1-INCH LENGTHS
- 10 FRESH BASIL LEAVES, THINLY SLICED
- 10 FRESH MINT LEAVES, THINLY SLICED
- 10 CILANTRO LEAVES, THINLY SLICED

1. Put the rice noodles in a large bowl, cover with boiling water, and let sit until softened, about a minute. Drain the noodles and set aside.

2. Put the rice paper wrappers in a bowl of hot water and let them soften for about a minute. Remove them from the water and set aside.

3. To assemble the crystal rolls, lay out a soaked rice paper wrapper and put a piece of the grilled tofu in the center. Sprinkle with the peanuts, then add 2 pieces of red pepper and 2 pieces of cucumber, and spread with equal amounts of the fresh herbs. Top with a handful of rice noodles, then fold in both sides of the roll.

NOTE: Round rice paper wrappers are available in health food stores and Asian markets.

NORI ROLLS

makes 5 rolls, serves 6

Nori rolls make a great light lunch on their own, but are sublime when served
with salad greens and grilled shiitake mushrooms. A sushi mat makes rolling
neat nori rolls much easier.

---

5 SHEETS OF TOASTED NORI SEAWEED
(DRIED LAVER)

2½ CUPS COOKED BROWN RICE
(SEE CHART, PAGE 210)

2½ TEASPOONS WASABI PASTE, OR
WASABI POWDER RECONSTITUTED
ACCORDING TO PACKAGE DIRECTIONS

1 AVOCADO, PEELED AND CUT INTO
SMALL CUBES

1 CUCUMBER, PEELED AND JULIENNED

3 CARROTS, PEELED AND JULIENNED

5 SCALLIONS, JULIENNED

1. Place a bamboo sushi rolling mat on a work surface so that the slats run horizontally. Place
a sheet of nori shiny side down on the mat. Moisten your hands with water and spread
¾ cup of brown rice evenly over the surface of the nori, leaving a 1½-inch-wide strip at
the top bare. Spread ½ teaspoon of wasabi paste horizontally about a third of the way up
the sheet and place a portion of each vegetable on top of the wasabi.

2. Starting at the bottom, use the sushi mat to roll the nori tightly and evenly away from you,
pressing down slightly as the roll turns. When you've reached the bare top edge, moisten it
slightly before sealing. Repeat with the remaining nori, rice, and vegetables.

3. Wrap each roll in plastic wrap and refrigerate until serving. To serve, cut each roll with a
sharp knife into 6 pieces, dipping the knife in water between cuts to keep the rice from
sticking.

CANDLE CAFE HAND ROLLS

makes 16 rolls, serves 8

We make hand rolls, Japanese style, by rolling tasty fillings with brown rice or sushi rice in sheets of toasted nori. They make delicious and beautiful appetizers or party fare when accompanied by Spicy Thai Dipping Sauce (page 161).

---

2 CUPS COOKED BROWN OR WHITE SUSHI RICE

4 LARGE SHEETS TOASTED NORI SEAWEED (DRIED LAVER), EACH CUT INTO 4 SQUARES

1 RECIPE UMEBOSHI-MARINATED TOFU, BELOW

1 RECIPE BURDOCK AND HIZIKI FILLING, OPPOSITE

Put 2 tablespoons rice in a long triangle shape on a nori square. Make a dent in the rice, place a strip of the tofu and about 1 tablespoon of the filling in the dent. Roll the nori over and around the tofu strip and filling to make a cone shape. Garnish the rolls with a scoop of Burdock and Hiziki Filling.

UMEBOSHI-MARINATED TOFU FILLING

makes 16 strips

---

3 TABLESPOONS SESAME OIL

1 TABLESPOON UMEBOSHI PASTE

2 TABLESPOONS MIRIN (JAPANESE RICE WINE)

2 TABLESPOONS SHOYU OR TAMARI SOY SAUCE

1 TABLESPOON FINELY CHOPPED SCALLION

½ POUND EXTRA-FIRM TOFU, WELL DRAINED AND CUT LENGTHWISE INTO QUARTERS

1. In a large bowl, mix together the sesame oil, umeboshi paste, mirin, shoyu or tamari soy sauce, 2 tablespoons water, and scallion. Pour over the tofu and let marinate for an hour.

2. Grill or broil the tofu quarters until browned, about 5 to 7 minutes per side. Remove from the heat and cut into thin strips. The filling is now ready to use in making hand rolls.

BURDOCK AND HIZIKI FILLING

makes 3 cups

---

1   TEASPOON SESAME OIL

1   10-INCH-LONG, 1-INCH-WIDE PIECE
    OF BURDOCK ROOT, PEELED AND
    JULIENNED

1   SMALL ONION, PEELED AND THINLY
    SLICED

2   TEASPOONS MINCED GARLIC

2   TEASPOONS PEELED AND MINCED
    FRESH GINGER

2   LARGE CARROTS, PEELED AND
    JULIENNED

2   TABLESPOONS HIZIKI, SOAKED IN
    WATER TO COVER FOR 10 MINUTES
    AND DRAINED

2   TABLESPOONS MIRIN

1   TABLESPOON SHOYU OR TAMARI SOY
    SAUCE

1   TABLESPOON BROWN RICE SYRUP

2   SCALLIONS, JULIENNED AND CUT
    INTO 1-INCH LENGTHS

1. Preheat the oven to 350°F.

2. Heat the oil in a sauté pan over medium-high heat. Add the burdock root and sauté for
   3 minutes. Add the onion, garlic, ginger, carrots, and hiziki; cover, and cook over low heat
   for an additional 20 minutes.

3. In a small bowl, mix together ¼ cup water, mirin, shoyu or tamari soy sauce, and brown
   rice syrup.

4. Toss the cooked burdock root mixture together on a baking sheet and spoon the mirin
   mixture over it. Bake for 20 minutes, or until most of the liquid has been absorbed, stirring
   occasionally.

5. Let cool and stir in the scallions. The filling is now ready to use in making hand rolls.

CROSTINI PLATTER

When we host a large party or cater an affair, we always make a crostini platter. To make crostini, we simply brush slices of French or Italian bread with a bit of olive oil and bake in the oven until they are lightly browned. Then we serve them with assorted dips, spreads, and even roasted garlic heads. The crostini platters look beautiful garnished with colorful chopped fresh vegetables and herbs.

BASIC CROSTINI

makes 32 slices, serves 8

1 LOAF FRENCH OR ITALIAN BREAD, CUT CROSSWISE INTO 32 SLICES

6 TABLESPOONS EXTRA-VIRGIN OLIVE OIL

1. Preheat the oven to 350°F.

2. Place the bread slices on a baking sheet and brush each slice with olive oil. Bake for 10 to 12 minutes, until golden brown.

VARIATION: Flavored crostini can be made by adding herbs or garlic to the olive oil. Flavored oils are also fantastic for making tasty crostini.

KALAMATA OLIVE AND SUN-DRIED TOMATO TAPENADE

makes about 1 cup

Tapenade, a thick paste made from sun-dried tomatoes, olives, and capers, is a wonderful condiment to serve with breads, crackers, and crudités.

1 CUP SUN-DRIED TOMATOES, SOAKED, DRAINED, AND QUARTERED

½ CUP PITTED KALAMATA OLIVES

1 TABLESPOON DRAINED CAPERS

1 GARLIC CLOVE, MINCED

2 TABLESPOONS EXTRA-VIRGIN OLIVE OIL

4 PARSLEY SPRIGS

Place all the ingredients in a food processor and blend until smooth. The tapenade will keep, covered, in the refrigerator for up to 4 days.

ROASTED PEPPER
AND OLIVE TAPENADE

makes 1½ cups, serves 6

This is a great-tasting, versatile tapenade that we serve not only with crostini but also with crudités and as a topping for steamed vegetables and vegetable burgers. The flavors mellow and improve if this is made a day ahead of time.

---

1 TO 2 TABLESPOONS EXTRA-VIRGIN OLIVE OIL

2 LARGE RED BELL PEPPERS, HALVED, STEMMED, SEEDED, AND DEVEINED

2 LARGE YELLOW BELL PEPPERS, HALVED, STEMMED, SEEDED, AND DEVEINED

⅓ CUP PITTED AND ROUGHLY CHOPPED GREEN OLIVES

⅓ CUP PITTED AND ROUGHLY CHOPPED BLACK OLIVES

1 TABLESPOON BOTTLED CAPERS, DRAINED

FRESHLY GROUND BLACK PEPPER

1. Preheat the oven to 350°F.

2. Toss the peppers with enough oil to coat, and bake until the peppers are soft, about 40 minutes. When cool enough to handle, peel the skins off the peppers and chop them.

3. Put the chopped peppers, olives, capers, and black pepper to taste in a food processor and process until smooth. Taste and adjust the seasoning. Cover and refrigerate for at least 1 hour and up to 3 days ahead of time.

4. Let the tapenade come to room temperature for 1½ to 2 hours before serving. Serve with crostini.

SUNFLOWER SEED SPREAD

makes 3 cups, serves 10 to 12

Nutty and delicious, this spread can be made ahead of time and is
excellent with crostini as well as on whole-grain toast points.

———————◆———————

2 CUPS RAW UNSALTED SUNFLOWER
SEEDS

1 POUND SILKEN TOFU

1 LEEK, WHITE PART ONLY, RINSED AND
FINELY DICED

FRESHLY GROUND BLACK PEPPER

⅓ CUP NUTRITIONAL YEAST FLAKES
(SEE NOTE)

5 TABLESPOONS SHOYU OR TAMARI SOY
SAUCE

1. Place the sunflower seeds in a large dry skillet and cook over medium heat, shaking the pan
occasionally, until lightly toasted, about 5 minutes.

2. Place the toasted sunflower seeds, tofu, leeks, pepper to taste, yeast flakes, and shoyu or
tamari soy sauce in a food processor and process until coarsely blended. With the motor
running, slowly add a bit of water through the feed tube, blending until incorporated. Use
only enough water to aid in blending and adjust the consistency. Cover and refrigerate for
up to one week.

3. Bring the spread to room temperature before serving. Serve with crostini.

NOTE: Rich in B vitamins and very nutritious, nutritional yeast flakes are available in
health food stores. They're great in gravies and salad dressings. They also add a great cheesy
flavor to popcorn.

VARIATION: Substitute pumpkin seeds for the sunflower seeds.

CARROT BUTTER BREAD SPREAD

makes 1½ cups, serves 6 to 8

Our Carrot Butter Bread Spread is much more than just a part of our crostini
platter. It's great as a snack with bread or muffins, or as a sandwich spread.
It's also a good first baby food—Joy's godson tasted it at age 7 months and
showed his hearty approval. For a great autumnal spread, use the same
amount of pumpkin or winter squash instead of carrot.

2 CUPS PEELED AND COARSELY
   CHOPPED CARROTS

2 CUPS PEELED AND COARSELY
   CHOPPED ONIONS

2 BAY LEAVES

1 TEASPOON EXTRA-VIRGIN OLIVE OIL

½ TEASPOON SEA SALT

1. Put all of the ingredients in a large stockpot, cover by about an inch of water, and bring to
   a boil. Reduce the heat and simmer, stirring frequently, until the carrots are tender, about 20
   to 25 minutes. Drain, remove the bay leaves, and set aside to cool.

2. Purée the carrots and onions in a food processor or blender until smooth. Cover and
   refrigerate. Store in an airtight container for up to 1 week.

HERB FARM DIP

makes 1 ½ cups, serves 6 to 8

This tangy, fresh, and delicious dip makes a fabulous party hors d'ouevre.
Whether served with crostini, crackers, or crudités, it's always a big crowd pleaser.
The generous amount of herbs creates an intensely flavored dip. Thanks to
Theresa Preston for sharing this recipe with us.

½ CUP COARSELY CHOPPED PARSLEY
LEAVES

½ CUP COARSELY CHOPPED FRESH
BASIL LEAVES

½ CUP COARSELY CHOPPED FRESH
CHIVES

½ CUP COARSELY CHOPPED FRESH DILL

½ CUP FINELY CHOPPED FRESH
BORAGE (SEE NOTE)

½ CUP FINELY CHOPPED FRESH
TARRAGON

1 SMALL RED ONION, PEELED AND
CHOPPED

2 TABLESPOONS WHOLE-GRAIN DIJON
MUSTARD

2 TABLESPOONS VEGAN MAYO
(PAGE 166)

8 OUNCES TOFU CREAM CHEESE,
PREFERABLY TOFUTTI BRAND

SEA SALT

FRESHLY GROUND BLACK PEPPER

1. Put the parsley, basil, chives, dill, borage, tarragon, onion, mustard, and Vegan Mayo in
a food processor and process. Add the cream cheese and a bit of salt and pepper and
process again until smooth, adding a bit more Vegan Mayo, if necessary. Taste and adjust
the seasonings.

2. The dip can be stored in the refrigerator, covered, for up to 1 week. Bring to room temperature before serving.

NOTE: If you can't find borage, substitute a small peeled and finely grated cucumber.

ROASTED GARLIC BULBS

serves 4

Crostini is luscious when spread with cloves of roasted garlic. We also serve whole heads of roasted garlic as an appetizer along with other dips and spreads.

---

4 WHOLE HEADS OF GARLIC

4 TABLESPOONS EXTRA-VIRGIN OLIVE OIL

1. Preheat the oven to 350°F.

2. Cut the tops off the heads of garlic so the top of each garlic clove is exposed. Drizzle each head with a tablespoon of olive oil and wrap in tinfoil. Bake until the garlic bulbs are soft, about 1 hour. Serve warm with crostini.

MISO-TAHINI SPREAD

makes 4 cups, serves 10 to 12

Miso-Tahini Spread has been in our cooking repertoire for more than fifteen years.
Used as a spread for chips and bread, or as a dip with raw vegetables,
it's an all-time favorite with our customers, who love it on corn bread.

1 CUP MELLOW MISO

1¼ CUPS SESAME TAHINI

1 CUP SHREDDED CARROTS

In a blender, combine 1¼ cups of water and the miso and blend until smooth. Transfer the
mixture to a bowl, stir in the tahini and carrots, and mix well to combine. The spread will
keep in the refrigerator, covered, for up to 7 days. Serve chilled or at room temperature.

HERBED TOFU SPREAD

makes about 2½ cups, serves 8

Our delicious Herbed Tofu Spread is a great spread for all types of sandwiches. We
especially like it in small tea sandwiches made with watercress and grilled mushrooms.

¼ CUP GARLIC CLOVES

2 TABLESPOONS EXTRA-VIRGIN
OLIVE OIL

1 POUND FIRM TOFU, BLANCHED AND
DRAINED

2 TABLESPOONS UMEBOSHI VINEGAR

2 TABLESPOONS LEMON JUICE

⅓ CUP CHOPPED PARSLEY

⅓ CUP STEMMED AND CHOPPED
WATERCRESS

1 TABLESPOON FINELY CHOPPED
FRESH TARRAGON OR BASIL

2 TEASPOONS FINELY CHOPPED FRESH
ROSEMARY, OR 1 TEASPOON DRIED

1 TEASPOON SEA SALT

FRESHLY GROUND BLACK PEPPER
TO TASTE

1. Preheat the oven to 350°F. Place the garlic in a small baking pan and cover with the olive
   oil. Bake until the garlic is softened and lightly browned, about 20 minutes.

2. Place the garlic and oil and the remaining ingredients in a blender and blend until smooth.
   The spread will keep in the refrigerator, covered, for up to 5 days. Serve chilled or at
   room temperature.

CAYENNE-CORN TORTILLA CHIPS WITH GUACAMOLE AND SALSAS

makes about 36 chips, serves 4 to 6

These chips are much lighter and have a richer corn flavor than commercial corn chips. They are delicious with salsa, Guacamole (below), and as a base for nachos made with soy cheese and pickled jalapeño slices.

———◆———

1 TABLESPOON EXTRA VIRGIN OLIVE OIL

¼ TEASPOON SEA SALT

1 TEASPOON PAPRIKA

PINCH OF CAYENNE

4 CORN TORTILLAS

1. Preheat the oven to 325°F.

2. Place the olive oil, salt, paprika, and cayenne in a large bowl and mix together well.

3. Cut each tortilla into 8 small wedges, then add them to the oil and spice mixture. Toss well to coat. Place the pieces on a baking sheet in a single layer. Bake for 15 to 20 minutes, until crisp. Taste and adjust the seasonings, adding a bit more salt or cayenne, if desired.

GUACAMOLE

makes about 1½ cups, serves 4 to 6

There are so many ways to make guacamole, but this is our hands-down favorite. The key to good guacamole is using ripe Haas avocados that give slightly when pressed. Although avocados are high in unsaturated fat, they are not fattening and contain a good amount of vitamin C and riboflavin.

———◆———

2 RIPE HAAS AVOCADOS, HALVED AND PITTED

2 TABLESPOONS FRESH LEMON JUICE

¼ CUP CHOPPED RED ONION

¼ CUP CHOPPED RED BELL PEPPER

1½ TABLESPOONS CHOPPED JALAPEÑO PEPPER

½ TEASPOON SEA SALT

⅓ CUP CHOPPED CILANTRO

CAYENNE-CORN TORTILLA CHIPS

1. Scoop the avocados and lemon juice into a large bowl and mash coarsely with a spoon.

2. Gently mix in the onion, red pepper, and jalapeño. Add the salt and cilantro. Taste and adjust the seasoning, if necessary. Best when served within an hour at room temperature with Cayenne-Corn Tortilla Chips.

MANGO AND PLUM TOMATO SALSA

makes about 2½ cups

This tasty and beautiful salsa, rich in vitamins A, C, and D, is a wonderful appetizer to serve in summer, when mangos and plum tomatoes are at their peak of freshness and flavor.

❖

4 FRESH PLUM TOMATOES, PEELED, SEEDED, AND FINELY DICED (SEE NOTE)

2 MANGOS, PEELED, SEEDED, AND FINELY DICED

1 MEDIUM RED ONION, PEELED AND FINELY DICED

½ CUP FINELY CHOPPED CILANTRO

JUICE OF 1 LIME

2 TO 3 DASHES OF HOT SAUCE

Place all the ingredients in a large bowl and mix together gently. Refrigerate for up to 6 hours. Let stand for 10 minutes before serving.

NOTE: To peel plum tomatoes, place the tomatoes in boiling water for a few seconds, then plunge into ice water. The skins will peel away easily with a knife.

PICO DE GALLO

makes about 4 cups

This chunky salsa makes a delicious appetizer served with Cayenne-Corn Tortilla Chips (page 33) or as a topping or condiment with all sorts of tacos, burritos, and enchiladas.

❖

6 LARGE TOMATOES, FINELY DICED

1 SMALL ONION, FINELY DICED

1 CUP FINELY CHOPPED CILANTRO

2 JALAPEÑOS, SEEDED AND COARSELY CHOPPED

1 TEASPOON SEA SALT

Place all the ingredients in a medium bowl and mix well. Serve Pico de Gallo at room temperature or refrigerate for at least 30 minutes and up to 6 hours before serving.

TOASTED PUMPKIN SEED SALSA

makes about 3 cups

This salsa is great served with chips as well as wraps and as a spicy
topping over brown rice or yellow basmati rice and beans.

- 1 DRIED ANCHO CHILE, SEEDED AND TORN INTO PIECES
- ½ CUP RAW PUMPKIN SEEDS
- 2 GARLIC CLOVES, CHOPPED
- 1 JALAPEÑO PEPPER, SEEDED AND COARSELY CHOPPED

- 3 TABLESPOONS SAFFLOWER OIL
- ½ ONION, COARSELY CHOPPED
- 1 28-OUNCE CAN ORGANIC CHOPPED TOMATOES
- 1 TEASPOON SEA SALT

1. Soak the chile pieces in a cup of warm water until softened, about 30 minutes. Drain and chop. Set aside.

2. Heat a large, dry skillet over high heat and add the pumpkin seeds, garlic, and jalapeño. Stir until toasted and the seeds begin to pop, about 1 to 2 minutes. Add the oil and onion and sauté, stirring, until the onion is translucent. Add the tomatoes and ancho chile, bring to a boil, reduce the heat, and simmer, uncovered, for 20 minutes. Stir in the salt. Remove from the heat and set aside to cool.

3. Transfer to a food processor and purée until smooth. This may have to be done in batches. The salsa will keep in the refrigerator, covered, for up to 5 days. Serve at room temperature.

SOUPS AND BROTHS

When the soul needs nurturing and the stomach needs nourishment, we turn to soup. We make a variety of soups and broths at the Candle Cafe, using filtered water and relying on the freshest ingredients we can find. Our soups are always cooked according to the seasons—Spring Vegetable Minestrone, summer-fresh Gazpacho, autumn harvest Butternut Squash Soup, and hearty winter Lentil Chowder are among our many favorites.

Broths, which are the basis of many of our soup and main-dish recipes, should always be made from the finest vegetables and most aromatic herbs available. These soups are subtly seasoned with sesame oil, miso, or shoyu or tamari soy sauce, and infused with both fresh and dried herbs for health benefits as well as flavor.

Feed your soul and your spirit with our favorite soup recipes from this chapter.

VEGETABLE BROTH

This broth is made by simply simmering vegetables and water together. It can be used on its own or as a base for soups, sauces, and stews. This nutritious broth is simple to make and a good thing to have on hand for a variety of recipes.

1 LARGE ONION, PEELED AND COARSELY CHOPPED

2 CARROTS, COARSELY CHOPPED

1 CELERY STALK, COARSELY CHOPPED

1 CUP SHIITAKE MUSHROOMS, PORTOBELLO MUSHROOM STEMS, OR WHOLE WHITE MUSHROOMS

1 PARSNIP, PEELED AND COARSELY CHOPPED

1 LEEK, WELL RINSED AND COARSELY CHOPPED

4 GARLIC CLOVES, PEELED

2 BAY LEAVES

½ CUP CHOPPED PARSLEY

5 THYME SPRIGS

5 BLACK PEPPERCORNS

1. Place all the ingredients with 8 cups of water in a large soup pot and bring to a boil. Reduce the heat and simmer, uncovered, for 1 hour, until the vegetables are very tender.

2. Let the broth cool slightly, then strain it, pressing hard on the vegetables to extract as much liquid as possible. Adjust the seasonings to taste. (This broth can be refrigerated for up to 6 days or frozen for up to 2 months.)

ROASTED VEGETABLE BROTH

serves 6 to 8

When vegetables are roasted and caramelized they become very rich
and mellow tasting, giving this variation on vegetable broth its marvelous flavor.
It's delicious on its own or as a soup or sauce base.

4 CARROTS, PEELED AND COARSELY
CHOPPED

1 LARGE ONION, PEELED AND
COARSELY CHOPPED

1 CELERY ROOT, PEELED AND
COARSELY CHOPPED

2 POTATOES, PEELED AND QUARTERED

2 PARSNIPS, PEELED AND COARSELY
CHOPPED

1 PORTOBELLO MUSHROOM, STEMMED
AND COARSELY CHOPPED

2 GARLIC CLOVES, PEELED

3 TABLESPOONS EXTRA-VIRGIN OLIVE
OIL

2 BAY LEAVES

½ TEASPOON WHOLE BLACK
PEPPERCORNS

5 THYME SPRIGS

2 TEASPOONS GROUND ALLSPICE

¼ CUP BROWN LENTILS, RINSED AND
SORTED

½ CUP DRY RED WINE

1. Preheat the oven to 400°F.

2. Place the carrots, onion, celery root, potatoes, parsnips, mushroom, and garlic on a baking
sheet. Sprinkle with olive oil, toss, and spread out the vegetables in an even layer. Roast
for 45 minutes, stirring occasionally.

3. In a large soup pot, combine the roasted vegetables with 3 quarts of water and add the
bay leaves, peppercorns, thyme sprigs, allspice, lentils, and wine. Bring to a boil, reduce the
heat, and simmer, uncovered, for 1 hour.

4. Let the broth cool slightly, then strain it, pressing hard on the vegetables to extract as much
liquid as possible. Adjust the seasonings to taste. (This broth can be refrigerated for up to
6 days or frozen for up to 2 months.)

SHIITAKE AND SCALLION BROTH

serves 6

This light broth is a wonderful appetizer that's a new favorite in the restaurant. The combination of dried and fresh shiitake mushrooms gives it true depth of flavor. Kombu is a type of Japanese seaweed, and it can be found in Asian and health food markets. We also consider this a healing broth, especially good to eat if you have a headache.

---

1 OUNCE DRIED SHIITAKE MUSHROOMS

1 3-INCH PIECE SLICED KOMBU (JAPANESE DRIED KELP)

12 FRESH SHIITAKE MUSHROOMS, THINLY SLICED

6 SCALLIONS, CHOPPED

3 TABLESPOONS SHOYU OR TAMARI SOY SAUCE

1. In a soup pot, soak the dried mushrooms in 6 cups of hot water for 30 minutes, until softened.

2. Add the kombu to the pot and bring to a boil. Reduce the heat and simmer for 5 minutes. Strain the stock, pressing firmly to extract as much liquid as possible. Add the fresh shiitake mushrooms, 5 chopped scallions, and the shoyu or tamari soy sauce to the strained broth and cook over medium heat until the mushrooms are tender, about 30 to 35 minutes.

3. Garnish the broth with the remaining chopped scallion and serve immediately.

LONG LIFE SOUP

serves 6 to 8

Chef Chris Fox introduced this appropriately named soup to the Candle.
Ginger, garlic, and cayenne are loaded with health benefits. They are said to
increase circulation and stimulate metabolism as well as build up immune
systems. Whether you're feeling a cold coming on or not, this is an excellent
soup to eat for your health and well-being.

———◆———

- 1 OUNCE DRIED SHIITAKE MUSHROOMS
- ½ CUP ARAME SEAWEED
- 1 TABLESPOON EXTRA-VIRGIN OLIVE OIL
- 1 YELLOW ONION, PEELED, HALVED, AND THINLY SLICED
- ¼ CUP MINCED GARLIC

- ½ CUP PEELED AND MINCED FRESH GINGER
- ½ CUP SHOYU OR TAMARI SOY SAUCE
- 1 TO 2 TEASPOONS CAYENNE, TO TASTE
- 2 TEASPOONS BROWN RICE VINEGAR
- 2 TEASPOONS ASIAN SESAME OIL

1. Place the dried shiitake mushrooms and the arame in 2 separate bowls and pour 4½ cups of hot water over each. Let sit for 15 minutes each. Drain the mushrooms and reserve the water. Thinly slice the mushrooms. Drain and rinse the arame and discard the water. Coarsely chop the arame.

2. Heat the oil in a sauté pan and cook the onion, garlic, and ginger until softened, about 10 minutes. Transfer to a soup pot and add the shoyu or tamari soy sauce, cayenne, vinegar, and sesame oil. Add the reserved mushroom water, mushrooms, arame, and an additional 4½ cups of water to the pot. Bring to a boil, reduce the heat, and simmer, uncovered, for 10 minutes. Serve immediately.

GINGER-LEMONGRASS
MISO SOUP

serves 6 to 8

Lemongrass, an essential ingredient in Thai cooking, adds a wonderful, refreshing flavor to soup, especially when combined with miso and ginger. Serve this delicious and revitalizing soup with a salad and simply cooked grains.

1 LEMONGRASS STALK, TRIMMED, PEELED, AND THINLY SLICED

1 TEASPOON SESAME OIL

1 MEDIUM YELLOW ONION, PEELED, HALVED, AND THINLY SLICED

2 TABLESPOONS MINCED FRESH GINGER

¾ CUP WHITE MISO

1 CUP ENOKI MUSHROOMS, FOR GARNISH

1 CUP THINLY SLICED SCALLIONS (GREEN PART ONLY), FOR GARNISH

1. In a stockpot, bring 8 cups of water and the lemongrass to a boil and simmer for 15 minutes; discard the lemongrass and strain, reserving the water.

2. Heat the oil in a sauté pan and cook the onion and ginger until the onion is translucent, about 10 minutes. Transfer to a soup pot and add the reserved water. Bring to a boil, reduce the heat, and simmer, uncovered, for 5 minutes. Turn off heat and stir in the miso.

3. Ladle the soup into bowls, garnish with the enoki mushrooms and scallions, and serve immediately.

MAGICAL MISO SOUP

serves 6 to 8

We have served miso soup since the Cafe's inception in 1984. Miso paste, a mainstay of Asian cuisine, is also known as fermented soybean paste and has a fairly thick consistency. It comes in a variety of flavors and colors and is found in Asian markets and health food stores. When making soup with miso, make sure that it is well dissolved in water but do not boil it—that diminishes the power of miso's nourishing enzymes. Our many miso soup fans say this soulful soup truly helps get them through the day. We hope it will help you, too.

1 MEDIUM ONION, PEELED AND THINLY SLICED

3 CARROTS, PEELED AND JULIENNED

⅛ SHEET OF WAKAME, SOAKED AND CHOPPED

1 CUP SWEET WHITE MISO

1 POUND TOFU, CUBED (OPTIONAL)

1. In a large soup pot, combine 6 cups of water, the onion, carrots, and wakame. Bring to a boil, reduce the heat, and simmer, uncovered, for 30 minutes.

2. Mix together the miso and 1 cup of water. Add the miso mixture to the soup and heat through, being careful not to bring to a boil. Stir the tofu cubes, if desired, into the soup and serve at once.

MISO

Miso can be mixed with water in a number of ways—with the back of a large spoon or with a mortar and pestle, among others. There is also a utensil called a Suribachi and Surikogí, which is similar to a mortar and pestle but is designed specifically for incorporating and dissolving water into miso.

SPRING VEGETABLE MINESTRONE

serves 6

What says spring better than a light soup made with fresh vegetables? When the weather turns warm we serve this lovely soup for lunch and dinner. It's full of tomatoes, scallions, garlic, and basil, among other good things.

---

3 TABLESPOONS EXTRA-VIRGIN OLIVE OIL

1 SMALL YELLOW ONION, PEELED AND FINELY DICED

5 SCALLIONS, MINCED

3 GARLIC CLOVES, PEELED AND THINLY SLICED

6 SMALL PLUM TOMATOES, FINELY DICED

1 MEDIUM ZUCCHINI, FINELY DICED

4 CUPS VEGETABLE BROTH (PAGE 38)

3 TABLESPOONS TOMATO PASTE

1 CUP COOKED NAVY BEANS, DRAINED

½ CUP CHOPPED FRESH BASIL LEAVES

1 BAY LEAF

½ TEASPOON FINELY CHOPPED FRESH THYME

½ TEASPOON FINELY CHOPPED FRESH ROSEMARY

1 TEASPOON SEA SALT

FRESHLY GROUND BLACK PEPPER

1. Heat the olive oil in a large soup pot and sauté the onion, scallions, garlic, tomatoes, and zucchini until tender, about 15 minutes.

2. Add the broth, tomato paste, beans, basil, bay leaf, thyme, rosemary, salt, and pepper to taste and bring to a boil. Reduce the heat and simmer, covered, over low heat, about 30 minutes.

3. Taste and adjust the seasonings.

TOMATO BASIL BISQUE

serves 6 to 8

This wholesome soup works best with super-fresh, juicy tomatoes, which
beautifully complement the basil and tofu. It makes a delicious summer lunch
when served with a green salad and whole wheat bread.

1 SMALL BEET, TRIMMED AND PEELED

2 TABLESPOONS EXTRA-VIRGIN
OLIVE OIL

½ CUP CHOPPED ONION

2 GARLIC CLOVES, PEELED AND THINLY
SLICED

½ CUP CHOPPED CELERY

6 CUPS VEGETABLE BROTH (PAGE 38)

12 SMALL TOMATOES, COARSELY
CHOPPED, OR 1 15-OUNCE CAN
WHOLE TOMATOES

1 CUP CHOPPED FRESH BASIL

1 TEASPOON DRIED THYME

½ TEASPOON DRIED OREGANO

1 CUP CUBED TOFU

SEA SALT

FRESHLY GROUND BLACK PEPPER

BASIL LEAVES, FOR GARNISH

1. Preheat the oven to 350°F. Put the beet on a baking sheet and bake until tender, 1 to
   1½ hours. When cool enough to handle, chop and set aside.

2. In a large soup pot, heat the olive oil and add the onion, garlic, and celery. Sauté for
   5 to 10 minutes, until tender, stirring occasionally.

3. Add the broth, tomatoes, basil, thyme, and oregano and bring to a boil. Reduce the heat
   and simmer for 20 to 25 minutes, stirring occasionally. Set aside to cool.

4. Transfer the soup, the cooked beet, and the tofu to a food processor or blender and blend
   until smooth. This may have to be done in batches. Return the soup to the pot, gently
   reheat, and add salt and pepper to taste. Garnish each serving with a whole basil leaf and
   serve at once.

SUMMER BORSCHT

serves 6 to 8

...aste their earthy best in late summer and that's when we love to make this easy
...t. Its vibrant red color is accentuated by the tomato and red bell pepper, and
its flavor is enhanced by the addition of a little orange juice. Not all beets are red,
though—if you select golden, pink, or white beets instead, the borscht will not have
its characteristic crimson hue, but its flavor will still be excellent.

---

2 CUPS VEGETABLE BROTH (PAGE 38)

6 MEDIUM BEETS, TRIMMED, PEELED, AND SLICED INTO ½-INCH-THICK SLICES (ABOUT 4 CUPS)

1 LARGE TOMATO, PEELED AND COARSELY CHOPPED

1 MEDIUM RED OR YELLOW BELL PEPPER, SEEDED, DEVEINED, AND COARSELY CHOPPED

1 BAY LEAF

1 TABLESPOON SAFFLOWER OIL

1 LARGE RED ONION, COARSELY CHOPPED

4 SCALLIONS, MINCED

½ CUP FINELY CHOPPED FLAT-LEAF PARSLEY

⅓ CUP FRESH ORANGE JUICE

SEA SALT AND FRESHLY GROUND BLACK PEPPER

TOFU-CILANTRO SOUR CREAM, FOR GARNISH (PAGE 167)

SNIPPED FRESH CHIVES, FOR GARNISH

1. In a large pot, combine 4 cups of water, the broth, beets, tomato, bell pepper, bay leaf and bring to a boil over high heat. Reduce the heat and simmer, partially covered, for 35 to 40 minutes, or until the vegetables are tender. Remove from the heat, discard the bay leaf, and set aside to cool.

2. Meanwhile, heat the oil in a small sauté pan over medium heat. Add the onion and scallions, cover, and cook, stirring occasionally, for about 10 minutes, or until tender. Stir the parsley into the vegetables just before removing from the heat. Stir the contents of the pan into the cooked beet mixture.

3. Drain the beet and onion mixture over a large bowl and reserve the cooking liquid.

4. Transfer half of the vegetables to a food processor fitted with the metal blade and purée. With the motor running, pour 1½ cups of the cooking liquid through the feed tube. When smooth, pour into a nonreactive bowl. Repeat with the remaining vegetables and 1½ cups of the cooking liquid. Save the remaining cooking liquid for another use (see Note).

5. Stir the orange juice into the soup. Season with salt and pepper and mix well. Cover and refrigerate for 2 to 3 hours, or until well chilled.

6. Stir the soup and adjust the seasoning, if necessary. Ladle into chilled soup bowls. Garnish each serving with a dollop of Tofu-Cilantro Sour Cream and a sprinkling of chives. Serve at once.

NOTE: The vegetable liquid makes an excellent drink for a midmorning pick-me-up and can also be used as a vegetable broth or a base for a vegetable sauce. It can be stored in the refrigerator or freezer.

GAZPACHO

serves 6 to 8

Refreshing and spicy gazpacho, full of fiber and vitamin C, is a perfect hot-weather soup and always a big hit with our summertime crowd. We take full advantage of the juicy, ripe tomatoes and garden-fresh cucumbers and peppers delivered daily by local farmers to our door throughout the season. You can do the same by visiting local farmer's markets for summertime produce.

4 MEDIUM TOMATOES, CORED AND CUT INTO 2-INCH CHUNKS

1 MEDIUM ONION, PEELED AND COARSELY CHOPPED

2 MEDIUM CUCUMBERS, PEELED, SEEDED, AND COARSELY CHOPPED

1 LARGE GREEN BELL PEPPER, SEEDED, DEVEINED, AND FINELY CHOPPED

1 LARGE RED BELL PEPPER, SEEDED, DEVEINED, AND FINELY CHOPPED

3/4 CUP FRESH LEMON JUICE

1/3 CUP SHOYU OR TAMARI SOY SAUCE

1/3 CUP BALSAMIC VINEGAR
HOT SAUCE

1/2 CUP FINELY CHOPPED CILANTRO

1/2 CUP FINELY CHOPPED FLAT-LEAF PARSLEY

1. In a nonreactive bowl, combine the tomatoes, onion, cucumbers, and peppers. Add the lemon juice, shoyu or tamari soy sauce, vinegar, and hot sauce to taste and stir to combine well. Transfer to a food processor or blender and blend until the consistency is fairly chunky. This may have to be done in batches. Stir in the cilantro and parsley, cover tightly, and refrigerate overnight.

2. To serve, ladle into chilled soup bowls or mugs.

SWEET CORN CHOWDER

serves 6

Freshly picked sweet corn is one of the many joys of high summer. We use it
variety of ways, but one of our favorite recipes is this light and flavorful chowder.

---

1   SMALL YELLOW ONION, PEELED AND
    FINELY CHOPPED

1   CARROT, PEELED AND FINELY
    CHOPPED

1   CELERY STALK, FINELY CHOPPED

½   CUP FINELY CHOPPED FLAT-LEAF
    PARSLEY

6   CUPS FRESH CORN KERNELS
    (FROM 8–10 EARS OF CORN)

1   TEASPOON SEA SALT
    FRESHLY GROUND BLACK PEPPER

½   TEASPOON MAPLE SYRUP (OPTIONAL)

1. Bring 5 cups of water to a boil in a large soup pot. Add the onion, carrot, celery, and
   parsley and cook, uncovered, over medium-high heat until the vegetables are tender,
   about 25 minutes. Stir in the corn and cook for an additional 5 minutes.

2. Transfer ⅓ of the chowder to a blender and blend until smooth. Return to the soup pot
   and stir.

3. Add the salt and pepper to taste. Taste and adjust the seasonings, adding the maple syrup
   if you desire a sweeter-tasting soup. Serve at once.

VELVETY CARROT
AND GINGER SOUP

serves 6

Freshly made foods, served directly from farm to table, have real nutritional density.
You can easily transform carrots, which are rich in vitamin A, into this velvety,
ginger-spiked soup. It's even more nutritious when you can find just-dug, farm-fresh
carrots from your local market. Served hot or cold, it is delicious either way.

1 TABLESPOON EXTRA-VIRGIN OLIVE OIL

3 MEDIUM ONIONS, PEELED AND
COARSELY CHOPPED

5 CUPS VEGETABLE BROTH (PAGE 38)

6 LARGE CARROTS, PEELED AND DICED

3 TABLESPOONS FINELY GRATED
FRESH GINGER

1 TEASPOON GROUND CINNAMON

1 TEASPOON GROUND CORIANDER

PINCH OF CAYENNE

SEA SALT AND FRESHLY GROUND
BLACK PEPPER, TO TASTE

½ CUP TOFU-CILANTRO SOUR CREAM
(PAGE 167), FOR GARNISH
(OPTIONAL)

½ CUP MINCED CHIVES, FOR GARNISH

1. In a stockpot set over medium heat, heat the olive oil. Add the onions and sauté for about
5 minutes, or until softened.

2. Add the broth, 1 cup of water, the carrots, and 2 tablespoons grated ginger. Bring to a boil,
reduce the heat, and simmer, partially covered, for about 20 minutes, until the carrots are
tender. Remove the pot from the heat and let the soup cool for about an hour.

3. In a food processor or blender, blend the soup with the remaining tablespoon of grated
ginger, the cinnamon, and coriander until very smooth. If a thinner consistency is desired,
add more broth or water. Season with the cayenne and salt and pepper to taste.

4. To serve warm, return the soup to the pot and reheat gently. If serving the soup cold,
cover and refrigerate for 2 to 3 hours, or until well chilled. Garnish each serving with
Tofu-Cilantro Sour Cream, if desired, and fresh chives.

BUTTERNUT SQUASH SOUP

serves 6 to 8

Butternut squash is an autumn treasure—especially when its sweet, golden flesh is
blended with onions and spices and made into this fragrant, creamy soup.
We call this soup the nectar of the gods.

---

3 MEDIUM BUTTERNUT SQUASH,
  PEELED, SEEDED, AND CUT INTO
  3-INCH CHUNKS

1 LARGE ONION, PEELED AND
  COARSELY CHOPPED

1½ CELERY STALKS, COARSELY CHOPPED

2 TABLESPOONS CHOPPED PARSLEY

½ TEASPOON SEA SALT

2 TO 3 TABLESPOONS MAPLE SYRUP
  (OPTIONAL)
  PARSLEY LEAVES, FOR GARNISH

¾ CUP TOASTED PUMPKIN SEEDS, FOR
  GARNISH (SEE NOTE)

1. In a large soup pot, put the squash, onion, and celery. Add 6 cups of water or vegetable stock and stir in the parsley and salt. Bring to a boil, cover, and reduce heat. Simmer for 20 minutes, until the vegetables are very tender. Remove from the heat and set aside to cool.

2. Transfer the soup to a food processor or blender and blend until smooth. This may have to be done in batches. Return the soup to the pot and reheat gently. Taste and adjust the seasonings, adding maple syrup if you prefer a sweeter-tasting soup. Garnish with the parsley leaves and toasted pumpkin seeds and serve at once.

NOTE: To toast pumpkin seeds, place the seeds in a dry skillet and sauté over medium heat until the seeds begin to brown and pop, about 3 minutes.

MUSHROOM AND WILD RICE SOUP

serves 6

Mushrooms and wild rice are a naturally delicious combination. We use both fresh and dried herbs in this soup because the combination adds so much extra flavor, aroma, and depth. A bowl of this earthy mix will nurture your body and soul.

½ CUP PLUS 4 TEASPOONS DRY WHITE WINE

2 GARLIC CLOVES, MINCED

1 SMALL WHITE ONION, PEELED AND DICED

½ LEEK, WHITE PART ONLY, RINSED AND FINELY CHOPPED

12 LARGE MUSHROOMS, SLICED

½ TEASPOON DRIED THYME

½ TEASPOON DRIED OREGANO

4 CUPS VEGETABLE BROTH (PAGE 38)

1 CUP COOKED WILD RICE (SEE CHART, PAGE 210)

2 TEASPOONS KUZU (SEE NOTE), OR 4 TEASPOONS UNBLEACHED FLOUR

FRESHLY GROUND BLACK PEPPER

CHOPPED FRESH THYME, FOR GARNISH

1. In a large saucepan, heat ½ cup white wine and bring to a simmer. Add the garlic, onion, and leek and simmer about 10 minutes, until the vegetables are tender.

2. Add the mushrooms, thyme, and oregano and simmer about 3 to 5 minutes, until the mushrooms are just tender. Add the broth, bring to a low boil, and simmer, uncovered, an additional 20 minutes. Stir in the cooked wild rice.

3. Dissolve the kuzu or flour in the remaining 4 teaspoons of white wine (or water) to form a thick paste. Stir it into the simmering soup. Bring back to a boil for 30 seconds, then remove from the heat.

4. Season the soup with pepper to taste, garnish with fresh thyme, and serve immediately.

NOTE: Kuzu is a natural thickening agent used in macrobiotic diets to aid in digestion.

CREAMY BROCCOLI SOUP

serves 6 to 8

We like to make this creamy broccoli soup for cold-weather lunches. It is thickened with a mixture of corn flour and water instead of cream, and has a wonderful texture. Broccoli, an antioxidant, is from the nutritious cruciferous family of vegetables, which also includes Brussels sprouts, cabbage, cauliflower, chard, kale, rutabagas, and turnips. All are high in fiber, vitamins, and minerals—so eat up!

6 CUPS VEGETABLE BROTH (PAGE 38) OR WATER

3 MEDIUM HEADS OF BROCCOLI (ABOUT 3 POUNDS), TRIMMED AND COARSELY CHOPPED

2 MEDIUM RED POTATOES, DICED

1 TABLESPOON EXTRA-VIRGIN OLIVE OIL

1 SMALL ONION, PEELED AND DICED

2 GARLIC CLOVES, MINCED

1 CELERY STALK, COARSELY CHOPPED

1 BUNCH OF PARSLEY, CHOPPED

½ CUP CORN FLOUR (SEE NOTE)

1 TEASPOON SEA SALT

FRESHLY GROUND BLACK PEPPER

1. In a large soup pot, combine the broth or water, broccoli, and potatoes and bring to a boil. Reduce the heat and simmer, uncovered, for 35 minutes, until the vegetables are very tender.

2. Meanwhile, heat the oil in a sauté pan and cook the onion, garlic, celery, and parsley for 10 minutes. Set aside.

3. Put the corn flour and 2 tablespoons of water in a small bowl and mix well until smooth.

4. Transfer the soup, the sautéed vegetables, and the corn flour mixture to a food processor or blender and blend until smooth. This may have to be done in batches.

5. Return the soup to the pot and gently reheat. Add the salt and pepper to taste and serve at once.

NOTE: Corn flour is finely ground cornmeal and is either yellow or white. It is available in supermarkets and health food stores.

MUSHROOM BARLEY SOUP

serves 6

When autumn in New York turns chilly, our customers clamor for Mushroom Barley
Soup, a great meal in a bowl. It's hearty but not heavy, and wonderful
when served with warm, crusty bread.

---

1 CARROT, PEELED AND COARSELY
CHOPPED

1 ONION, PEELED AND COARSELY
CHOPPED

1 CELERY STALK, COARSELY CHOPPED

6 CUPS VEGETABLE BROTH (PAGE 38)

1½ CUPS THINLY SLICED FRESH
MUSHROOMS

1 CUP UNCOOKED BARLEY

2 TABLESPOONS CHOPPED PARSLEY

½ CUP CHOPPED FRESH DILL

1½ TABLESPOONS SEA SALT

1 TEASPOON FRESHLY GROUND BLACK
PEPPER

1. In a large soup pot, put the carrot, onion, celery, and broth and bring to a boil. Reduce the
heat and simmer, uncovered, for 20 minutes.

2. Add the mushrooms, barley, parsley, dill, salt, and pepper to the soup and simmer, uncovered,
for an additional 30 minutes, or until the barley is just tender. Taste, adjust the seasonings,
and serve immediately.

CANDLE CAFE'S WORLD-FAMOU
SPLIT PEA SOUP

serves 6

Traditional split pea soup is often a heavy affair. Our restaurant's version
is simply made with split peas, fresh vegetables, and herbs and requires
very little cooking time—easy, light, and delicious.

2½ CUPS SPLIT PEAS

1 LARGE ONION, PEELED AND
CHOPPED

3 CARROTS, PEELED AND CHOPPED

2 CELERY STALKS, CHOPPED

PINCH OF FRESH ROSEMARY

PINCH OF FRESH THYME

PINCH OF FRESH OREGANO

PINCH OF SEA SALT

FRESHLY GROUND BLACK PEPPER

1. In a large stockpot, put 6 cups of water and bring to a boil over high heat. Add the split peas, onion, carrots, celery, and herbs. Stir and bring to a boil again.

2. Reduce the heat and simmer, uncovered, until the peas and vegetables are tender, about an hour. If you prefer a creamy soup, transfer half of the mixture to a food processor or blender, blend until smooth, return it to the soup, and mix well to combine.

3. Season to taste with salt and pepper and serve immediately.

MIXED VEGETABLE
MATZO BALL SOUP

serves 10 to 12

version of "chicken" soup, or Jewish penicillin, is a healthy blend of leeks, garlic,
lots of fresh vegetables, and herbs. We always have plenty on hand, because,
just like the original version, it's good for what ails you.

VEGETABLE SOUP STOCK

2 LEEKS, RINSED AND COARSELY
CHOPPED

4 GARLIC CLOVES, PEELED

5 SHALLOTS OR 2 SMALL ONIONS,
PEELED AND QUARTERED

4 CARROTS, PEELED AND COARSELY
CHOPPED

2 PARSNIPS, PEELED AND COARSELY
CHOPPED

2 CELERY STALKS, COARSELY CHOPPED

1 ¼-INCH PIECE OF KOMBU, RINSED

⅓ TO ½ CUP FRESH LEMON JUICE

6 PARSLEY SPRIGS, OR 1 TABLESPOON
DRIED PARSLEY

6 DILL SPRIGS, OR 1 TABLESPOON
DRIED DILL

1 TEASPOON EACH: DRIED THYME,
BASIL, OREGANO, MARJORAM, AND
ROSEMARY

2 TO 3 TEASPOONS HERBAMARE (SEE
NOTE) OR 1 TEASPOON SEA SALT

1 TEASPOON WHITE PEPPER
(OPTIONAL)

VEGETABLE MATZO BALLS

2 CUPS PEELED AND GRATED
POTATOES

½ CUP LUKEWARM SPRING WATER

1 TEASPOON SEA SALT

1 TABLESPOON EXTRA-VIRGIN OLIVE OIL

1 TABLESPOON FRESH OR DRIED DILL

1 TABLESPOON FINELY CHOPPED
PARSLEY

1 TEASPOON GARLIC POWDER

1 TEASPOON ONION POWDER

1 ¼ CUPS MATZO MEAL

12 SPRIGS FRESH PARSLEY, FOR
GARNISH

1 CARROT, FINELY CHOPPED AND
BLANCHED, FOR GARNISH
(OPTIONAL)

1 CELERY STALK, COARSELY CHOPPED,
FOR GARNISH (OPTIONAL)

1. Make the soup: In a large soup pot, put 3 quarts of water, the leeks, garlic, shallots or
onions, carrots, parsnips, celery, kombu, lemon juice, parsley, dill, and dried herbs. Bring to
a boil, reduce the heat, and simmer, uncovered, for 35 minutes.

2. Add the Herbamare or salt and white pepper, if desired, and simmer an additional 15 minutes.

3. Let the broth cool slightly, then strain it, pressing hard on the vegetables to extract as much
liquid as possible. You can reserve the carrots, celery, and parsnips to serve in the broth if
you wish or add fresh vegetables for extra crunch.

4. Taste and adjust the seasonings. (At this point, the broth can be refrigerated for up to a week or frozen for up to a month.)

5. Make the matzo balls: In a medium bowl, mix together the potatoes, water, sea salt, olive oil, dill, parsley, garlic powder, and onion powder. Gradually add 1 cup of the matzo meal to the mixture. Spread the remaining ¼ cup of matzo meal in a thin layer on a plate.

6. With moistened hands, form the matzo mixture into 1-inch balls and place them on the plate of matzo meal.

7. Bring the soup to a gentle boil and drop in the matzo balls. Cover and simmer for 30 to 40 minutes. Remove the matzo balls with a slotted spoon.

8. Serve the matzo balls with the soup, parsley, and carrots and celery, if desired, ladled over them.

NOTE: Herbamare is a blend of organically grown herbs and vegetables steeped in sea salt. It is sold in small packages in health food stores.

ONION SOUP

serves 6

It is said that foods from one's childhood conjure up powerful memories. Joy's mom
used to make onion soup in her special soup crocks, and today Joy makes hers in
those very same bowls, sustaining a tradition while nurturing friends and family.
Her delicious and satisfying version is made with onions, shallots, croutons,
and a slice of soy cheese—mmmmm good!

2   TABLESPOONS EXTRA-VIRGIN
    OLIVE OIL

3   LARGE ONIONS, HALVED AND THINLY
    SLICED

4   SHALLOTS, FINELY CHOPPED

6   CUPS VEGETABLE BROTH (PAGE 38)

    PINCH OF SEA SALT

    PINCH OF DRIED OREGANO

    PINCH OF DRIED THYME

    FRESHLY GROUND BLACK PEPPER

1   TABLESPOON SHOYU OR TAMARI
    SOY SAUCE

2   CUPS CROUTONS (PAGE 171)

6   SLICES OF SOY CHEESE

1. In a large skillet over medium-low heat, heat the olive oil. Add the onions and shallots and
   sauté until they are soft and golden, about 30 to 35 minutes.

2. In a soup pot, bring broth to a boil and add the sautéed onions and shallots, sea salt,
   oregano, thyme, and pepper to taste. Stir in the shoyu or tamari soy sauce. Reduce the heat
   and simmer for 45 minutes. Taste and adjust the seasonings.

3. Ladle the soup into 6 onion soup crocks or ovenproof bowls (see Note). Top each with
   croutons and place a slice of cheese over each serving. Place under the broiler until the
   cheese melts, or bake until the cheese has melted and the soup is bubbly. Serve at once.

NOTE: If you don't have ovenproof bowls, just melt the cheese over the croutons in a
350°F oven for 3 to 5 minutes, then place them over the soup just before serving.

POTATO-LEEK SOUP

serves 8 to 10

We are big fans of leeks. Their subtle flavor is excellent in soups, sauces, and stews and they also taste great simply sautéed in olive oil. Fresh leeks are available almost all year nowadays, but this soup is a special favorite in autumn and winter.

4 POTATOES, PEELED AND COARSELY CHOPPED

2 LEEKS, WHITE AND PALE GREEN PARTS ONLY, RINSED AND FINELY CHOPPED

2 LARGE ONIONS, PEELED AND FINELY CHOPPED

4 CARROTS, PEELED AND FINELY CHOPPED

4 CELERY STALKS, FINELY CHOPPED

1 TEASPOON DRIED OR 1 TABLESPOON CHOPPED FRESH PARSLEY

1 TEASPOON SEA SALT

FRESHLY GROUND BLACK PEPPER

1. In a large soup pot, put 7 cups of water, the potatoes, leeks, onions, carrots, and celery. Bring to a boil and add the parsley, sea salt, and pepper to taste. Reduce the heat and simmer, uncovered, for 30 minutes, until the vegetables are very tender. Remove from the heat and set aside to cool.

2. Transfer the soup to a food processor or blender and blend until smooth. This may have to be done in batches. Return the soup to the pot and gently reheat. Taste, adjust the seasonings, and serve at once.

SWEET POTATO AND WATERCRESS SOUP

serves 4 to 6

Orange sweet potatoes and deep green watercress are a marvelous combination in soups or salads. This soup is a good starter for any meal.

2 TABLESPOONS EXTRA-VIRGIN OLIVE OIL

1 LARGE ONION, PEELED AND FINELY CHOPPED

5 GARLIC CLOVES, PEELED AND THINLY SLICED

2 MEDIUM SWEET POTATOES, PEELED AND DICED

1 SMALL WHITE POTATO, PEELED AND DICED

1 BUNCH OF WATERCRESS, RINSED AND STEMMED

¼ TEASPOON SEA SALT

1. In a skillet or sauté pan over medium heat, heat the olive oil. Add the onion and garlic and sauté until the onion is soft, about 10 minutes.

2. In a large soup pot, put 6 cups of water and the potatoes and stir in the sautéed onion and garlic. Bring to a boil, reduce the heat, and simmer, uncovered, for about 40 minutes, until the potatoes are tender.

3. Put a third of the soup and a third of the watercress in a blender and blend until smooth. Add an additional third of the soup and the watercress and repeat. Stir in the remaining soup mixture, the remaining watercress, and the sea salt. Return the soup to the pot and gently reheat. Taste, adjust the seasonings, and serve at once.

CURRIED POTATO-SPINACH SOUP

serves 8

This is a good soup to serve on a crisp autumn afternoon. It's delicious, with a spicy cayenne kick. It's one of our restaurant's all-time favorites.

¼ CUP EXTRA-VIRGIN OLIVE OIL

½ ONION, PEELED AND COARSELY CHOPPED

1 TABLESPOON CURRY POWDER

1 TEASPOON FENNEL SEEDS

1 TEASPOON GROUND CORIANDER

1 TEASPOON TURMERIC

1 TEASPOON GROUND CUMIN

¼ TEASPOON CAYENNE

2 GARLIC CLOVES, MINCED

1 CELERY STALK, CHOPPED

4 MEDIUM YUKON GOLD POTATOES, PEELED AND CHOPPED

1 CUP CHOPPED CAULIFLOWER FLORETS

3 QUARTS VEGETABLE BROTH (PAGE 38) OR WATER

1 BUNCH OF SPINACH, RINSED, STEMMED, AND COARSELY CHOPPED

1 TO 2 TABLESPOONS SEA SALT, TO TASTE

½ CUP CHOPPED CILANTRO, FOR GARNISH

1. In a soup pot over medium heat, heat the oil. Add the onion, curry powder, fennel seeds, coriander, turmeric, cumin, and cayenne. Sauté until the onion is translucent, about 5 minutes. Add the garlic and celery and sauté about 2 minutes, being careful the garlic doesn't burn. Add the potatoes and cauliflower and stir to coat with the spices. Add the broth or water. Bring to a boil, reduce the heat, and simmer, uncovered, until the vegetables are tender, about 45 minutes. Stir in the spinach. Remove from the heat and set aside to cool.

2. Transfer the soup to a food processor or blender and blend until smooth. This may have to be done in batches.

3. Return the soup to the pot and gently reheat. Add the salt to taste, garnish with cilantro, and serve at once.

BLACK BEAN SOUP

serves 6 to 8

We serve fabulous Black Bean Soup at Candle Cafe. Here is our basic recipe, which is terrific on its own, but feel free to add your own toppings to the soup. Delicious additions such as sautéed peppers, freshly chopped tomatoes and cilantro, roasted corn, and even grilled mangos can be added to the soup. Let your imagination, and what's fresh at the market, be your guide.

2½ CUPS BLACK BEANS, RINSED AND PICKED OVER

1 1-INCH PIECE OF KOMBU

8 CUPS VEGETABLE BROTH (PAGE 38)

1 SMALL YELLOW ONION, PEELED AND DICED

1 CELERY STALK, DICED

1 CARROT, PEELED AND DICED

1 TEASPOON FRESH OR DRIED OREGANO

1 TEASPOON CHOPPED FRESH OR DRIED ROSEMARY

1 TEASPOON FRESH OR DRIED THYME

SEA SALT

FRESHLY GROUND BLACK PEPPER

TOFU-CILANTRO SOUR CREAM (PAGE 167), FOR GARNISH

1. Put the black beans and the kombu in a large pot or bowl and cover by about 2 inches of cold water. Soak the beans for at least 6 to 8 hours or up to overnight. Drain, discard the kombu, and set the beans aside.

2. Put the beans, broth, onion, celery, carrot, oregano, rosemary, and thyme in a large soup pot and bring to a boil. Reduce the heat and simmer for approximately 45 minutes, until the beans are softened. Season to taste with sea salt and pepper. Taste, adjust the seasonings, and serve.

LENTIL CHOWDER

serves 4 to 6

We love to make this slow-cooking chowder for a winter lunch or dinner. It is rich and satisfying and a cinch to make. This Lentil Chowder is also hearty enough to be served as a stew on a bed of grains.

1 CUP BROWN, GREEN, OR RED LENTILS, RINSED

1 MEDIUM ONION, COARSELY CHOPPED

1 MEDIUM POTATO, PEELED AND COARSELY CHOPPED

1 MEDIUM BUTTERNUT SQUASH, PEELED, SEEDED, AND COARSELY CHOPPED

1 CELERY STALK, COARSELY CHOPPED

1 CARROT, PEELED AND COARSELY CHOPPED

1 TOMATO, SEEDED AND DICED

1½ TABLESPOONS TOMATO PASTE

2 TEASPOONS DRIED THYME

FRESHLY GROUND BLACK PEPPER

1. In a large soup pot, combine the lentils, 4 cups of water, the onion, potato, squash, celery, carrot, tomato, tomato paste, thyme, and pepper to taste. Slowly bring to a boil, reduce the heat, and simmer for about 1½ hours over very low heat, stirring occasionally. Add a bit more water if the soup seems to be getting too thick.

2. Taste, adjust the seasonings, and serve at once.

NOTE: You can also cook this soup in a Crock-Pot for approximately 3 hours over high heat.

SALADS

Over the past few years, salads have evolved from plain lettuce topped with bland oil and vinegar or heavy dressing to delightful combinations of greens, roasted vegetables, grains, and sprouts tossed with dressings and vinaigrettes made from a wide variety of ingredients.

Salads are a mainstay of the Candle Cafe menu. We serve all types of fresh salads year-round, using the finest ingredients made available to us by our local farmers and suppliers. You can do the same thing by exploring your local farmer's market, picking out the produce that looks best, and improvising a salad using one of the recipes in this chapter as your guide.

Most of the recipes in this chapter make 2 cups of dressing—plenty for the salad and then some. Keep the extra dressing in your refrigerator to spice up grains, beans, and vegetables.

CAESAR SALAD WITH HERBED CROUTONS AND NORI DRESSING

serves 6 to 8

Our version of this classic salad is a favorite of Mark Felix, a chef at
New York's world-renowned Plaza Hotel. He recently served it at a dinner
there to benefit the Farm Sanctuary. Hail, Caesar and Mark!

2 HEADS OF ROMAINE LETTUCE

HERBED CROUTONS

¼ CUP EXTRA-VIRGIN OLIVE OIL

½ TEASPOON DRIED THYME

½ TEASPOON DRIED OREGANO

SEA SALT AND FRESHLY GROUND
BLACK PEPPER

2 CUPS DAY-OLD 1-INCH BREAD CUBES

NORI DRESSING (RECIPE FOLLOWS)

DASH OF TOASTED DULSE (SEE NOTE)

1. Tear the lettuce into small pieces, put in a large salad bowl, and set aside.

2. Preheat the oven to 350°F. In a large bowl, whisk together the olive oil, thyme, oregano, and salt and pepper to taste. Toss the bread cubes with the olive oil mixture until well coated. Place in a single layer on a baking sheet and bake until golden brown, 15 to 20 minutes. Remove and set aside to cool.

3. Toss the lettuce and Nori Dressing together. Add the croutons and toss again. Sprinkle the salad with the toasted dulse.

NOTE: Dulse is a sea vegetable that is rich in minerals. It has a slightly salty, fishy flavor and is excellent on salads. It is also available in dried flake form. Dulse can be bought in health food stores and Asian markets. To toast the dulse, pull it apart and put several strands on a baking sheet. Bake in a 350°F oven for 15 minutes, or until dry. Crumble into flakes and store in an airtight container.

NORI DRESSING

makes 2 cups

¼ CUP EXTRA-VIRGIN OLIVE OIL

½ CUP SOY MILK

½ POUND SILKEN TOFU

1 TABLESPOON CAPERS

1 TABLESPOON DIJON MUSTARD

¼ CUP FRESH LEMON JUICE

1 TABLESPOON SHOYU OR TAMARI SOY SAUCE

½ TEASPOON HOT SAUCE

2 GARLIC CLOVES, MINCED

1 SHEET OF NORI, SHREDDED

Place the olive oil, soy milk, tofu, capers, mustard, and lemon juice in a blender and blend until smooth. Add the shoyu or tamari soy sauce, hot sauce, garlic, and shredded nori and pulse again until smooth. The dressing will keep, covered, in the refrigerator for up to a week.

OUR DRESSINGS AND VINAIGRETTES

Our recipes for dressings and vinaigrettes yield generous amounts. Not only do we use them in salads, but we like to have plenty of extra on hand for a number of uses. We use them for dips for crudités, crisps, and toasts. They are also very good to use as marinades and are excellent when drizzled over steamed vegetables, rice, and grains. All of the dressings and vinaigrettes can be made well ahead of time and stored in the refrigerator for days.

CANDLE COBB SALAD WITH CARROT-GINGER DRESSING

serves 2 as an entrée, 4 to 6 as a side dish

This classic salad is great to eat when you're craving a dish that's rich in variety and texture. We also incorporate tofu salad into a number of other recipes, and it's delicious on its own as well.

TOFU SALAD

- 1 POUND FIRM TOFU, CUBED
- 2 TABLESPOONS CHOPPED FRESH DILL
- 2 TABLESPOONS CHOPPED PARSLEY
- 4 SCALLIONS, FINELY CHOPPED
- ¼ TABLESPOON WHITE MISO
- ½ CUP TAHINI
- 1 TEASPOON HERBAMARE OR SEA SALT
- 1 PINCH OF PEPPER
- 1 TEASPOON FRESH LEMON JUICE
- 1 CELERY STALK, CHOPPED
- ½ CUP SHREDDED CARROTS

- 4 CUPS MESCLUN
- 1 LARGE TOMATO, CUT INTO 8 SLICES
- 3 THIN SLICES OF CHEDDAR SOY CHEESE
- 4 TO 5 BUTTON MUSHROOMS, THINLY SLICED
- 1 CUP CROUTONS (PAGE 171)
- 1 CUP SHREDDED CARROTS
- 8 SLICES OF GRILLED OR SAUTÉED TEMPEH BACON (OPTIONAL)
- ½ CUP CARROT-GINGER DRESSING (RECIPE FOLLOWS)

1. Bring a pot of water to a boil. Add the tofu, cook for 1 minute, and drain immediately.

2. Mix together the blanched tofu, dill, parsley, scallions, miso, tahini, Herbamare, pepper, and lemon juice in a large glass bowl. Fold in the celery and carrots until well combined.

3. To assemble the salad, divide the mesclun among the plates. Using a small scoop, put ¼ cup of tofu salad in the center of each. Then place the tomato slices, cheese, mushrooms, croutons, carrots, and bacon (evenly divided) in a circle around the tofu. Drizzle the salad with Carrot-Ginger Dressing and serve with additional dressing on the side.

CARROT-GINGER DRESSING

makes 3 cups

We are famous for our Carrot-Ginger Dressing. It is good on everything and we've
seen it on everything. Our chefs produce about 20 gallons a week in the restaurant
and all of our customers want the recipe. Here it is.

¼ CUP MINCED FRESH GINGER

2 GARLIC CLOVES, SLICED

¼ CUP DICED ONIONS

2 CUPS PEELED AND SHREDDED
CARROTS

2 TABLESPOONS APPLE JUICE

1 TEASPOON TOASTED SESAME OIL,
OR TO TASTE

1 CUP SAFFLOWER OIL

½ TO ¾ CUP APPLE CIDER VINEGAR

Put the ginger, garlic, onions, and carrots in a food processor and process until finely
chopped. Transfer to a blender. Add the apple juice, sesame oil, safflower oil, and vinegar
and blend until well combined. Taste and adjust the seasonings. The dressing will keep in
the refrigerator, tightly covered, for up to 10 days.

CHOPPED SALAD WITH CREAMY CHIPOTLE RANCH DRESSING

serves 4 to 6

This is a great-tasting and great-looking salad, with a mélange of freshly chopped vegetables over a bed of radicchio leaves and sliced tomatoes. We like to serve it for a summer afternoon lunch or on a large platter for an outdoor buffet.

2 CUPS MIXED CHOPPED ROMAINE AND GREEN AND RED OAK LEAF LETTUCE

1 CUCUMBER, PEELED AND DICED

1 RED BELL PEPPER, SEEDED, DEVEINED, AND DICED

2 CELERY STALKS, DICED

1 RED ONION, PEELED AND DICED

2 CARROTS, PEELED AND DICED

CREAMY CHIPOTLE RANCH DRESSING (RECIPE FOLLOWS)

1 SMALL HEAD OF RADICCHIO

2 MEDIUM TOMATOES, CUT INTO WEDGES

WATERCRESS SPRIGS, FOR GARNISH (OPTIONAL)

1. Toss the lettuce, cucumber, pepper, celery, onion, and carrots with about ¾ cup dressing to coat and hold the vegetables together.

2. Place 2 or 3 large radicchio leaves on each salad plate and surround them with the tomato wedges. Scoop the chopped salad in the center of the radicchio leaves and top with the watercress sprigs, if using. Spoon a bit more dressing over the salad if desired.

CREAMY CHIPOTLE RANCH DRESSING

makes about 2 cups

We love this sensational smoky, creamy dressing and use it in many different ways. In addition to chopped salad, we serve it over baked potatoes, as a sandwich spread, and as a dip for chips and vegetables. Try it—you'll like it.

½ POUND SILKEN TOFU

¼ CUP SAFFLOWER OIL

½ TEASPOON NUTRITIONAL YEAST

2 TABLESPOONS DRAINED CAPERS

1 TABLESPOON FRESH LEMON JUICE

1½ TEASPOONS BROWN RICE SYRUP

1 TABLESPOON APPLE CIDER VINEGAR

1 DRIED CHIPOTLE PEPPER

2 TABLESPOONS CHOPPED ONION

1 SHALLOT, PEELED AND MINCED

½ TEASPOON SEA SALT

½ TEASPOON CHILI POWDER

¼ TEASPOON PAPRIKA

1 GARLIC CLOVE, MINCED

Place all of the ingredients in a blender and blend until smooth. Taste and adjust the seasonings. The dressing will keep in the refrigerator, covered, for up to a week. Serve chilled.

GREEK SALAD WITH HERBED VINAIGRETTE

serves 6 to 8

We love to sit outdoors in a sunny spot and eat this with friends and family. For a true Mediterranean treat, serve it with a large Mezze Platter (page 14) and pita bread.

½ POUND TOFU

2 TABLESPOONS SEA SALT

2 TEASPOONS FRESH LEMON JUICE

2 SMALL HEADS OF ROMAINE LETTUCE, TORN INTO BITE-SIZED PIECES

1 LARGE CUCUMBER, PEELED AND CUT INTO 1-INCH CHUNKS

1 TOMATO, PEELED AND CUT INTO 1-INCH CHUNKS

1 SMALL RED ONION, HALVED AND THINLY SLICED

1 RED BELL PEPPER, SEEDED, DEVEINED, AND DICED

HERBED VINAIGRETTE (RECIPE FOLLOWS)

¼ CUP BLACK OLIVES, SUCH AS KALAMATA OR NIÇOISE, FOR GARNISH

1. Bring a pot of water to a boil. Add the tofu, cook for 1 minute, and drain immediately. When cool enough to handle, cut the tofu into 6 pieces.

2. Put the tofu in a large nonreactive bowl and cover with a quart of water, the salt, and lemon juice and marinate in the refrigerator overnight. Drain.

3. Put the lettuce, cucumber, tomato, onion, and pepper in a large salad bowl. Toss with the Herbed Vinaigrette and garnish with the olives. Crumble the tofu "feta" on top of the salad.

HERBED VINAIGRETTE

makes 3 cups

Here is our classic vinaigrette, which we serve with Greek Salad. It's also very good as a light sauce for orzo pasta and as a marinade for grilled vegetables, tofu, and seitan. The possibilities are endless.

---

2 CUPS EXTRA-VIRGIN OLIVE OIL

1 CUP WHITE WINE VINEGAR

1½ TEASPOONS SEA SALT

1 TEASPOON FRESHLY GROUND BLACK PEPPER

¼ CUP FRESH LEMON JUICE

¼ CUP CHOPPED PARSLEY

2 TABLESPOONS CHOPPED FRESH OR 1 TABLESPOON DRIED OREGANO

2 TABLESPOONS CHOPPED FRESH OR 1 TABLESPOON DRIED TARRAGON

2 TABLESPOONS CHOPPED FRESH OR 1 TEASPOON DRIED THYME

1 TABLESPOON WHOLE-GRAIN DIJON MUSTARD

Put all of the ingredients in a blender and blend until well combined. Taste and adjust the seasonings. The dressing will keep in the refrigerator, tightly covered, for up to 10 days.

SPINACH SALAD WITH WARM MUSHROOMS, PINE NUTS, AND BALSAMIC VINEGAR

serves 6

We enjoy making this wonderful, warm salad as an appetizer for a cold-weather
dinner. The woodsy flavor of sautéed cremini and shiitake mushrooms works
very well with tart lemon juice, capers, and balsamic vinegar.

- 5 TABLESPOONS EXTRA-VIRGIN OLIVE OIL
- ¼ POUND CREMINI MUSHROOMS, STEMMED AND THINLY SLICED
- ¼ POUND SHIITAKE MUSHROOMS, STEMMED AND THINLY SLICED
- 2 GARLIC CLOVES, MINCED
- 2 TABLESPOONS PITTED AND FINELY MINCED KALAMATA OLIVES
- 2 TABLESPOONS DRAINED CAPERS

- 2 TABLESPOONS FRESH LEMON JUICE
- 1 TABLESPOON BALSAMIC VINEGAR
- 2 BUNCHES OF FRESH SPINACH, TRIMMED, RINSED, AND PATTED DRY
- 1 SMALL RED ONION, PEELED, HALVED, AND THINLY SLICED
  SEA SALT
  FRESHLY GROUND BLACK PEPPER
- ¼ CUP TOASTED PINE NUTS (SEE NOTE)

1. In a sauté pan over medium-high heat, heat 3 tablespoons of the oil. Add the mushrooms and cook, stirring frequently, about 5 minutes. Reduce the heat to medium and stir in the garlic, olives, capers, lemon juice, and vinegar. Simmer for 5 minutes.

2. Meanwhile, tear the spinach into bite-sized pieces and toss with the red onion and remaining olive oil in a large bowl. Season to taste with the salt and pepper. Add the warm mushroom mixture to the spinach and toss again until thoroughly blended. Divide the salad among 6 plates and sprinkle each serving with the toasted pine nuts. Serve at once.

NOTE: To toast the pine nuts, spread them on a baking sheet and toast in a preheated 350°F oven or toaster oven for about 3 minutes, until golden brown. Shake the pan once or twice for even toasting. Slide the nuts off the baking sheet to stop the cooking and let them cool.

ARUGULA AND PEAR SALAD WITH RASPBERRY VINAIGRETTE

serves 6 to 8

This is a very elegant but simple salad, served with piquant
Raspberry Vinaigrette and crunchy pecans.

---

6 CUPS ARUGULA, TOUGH STEMS
REMOVED, RINSED AND DRIED

3 PEARS, PEELED AND THINLY SLICED

¼ CUP WHOLE PECANS

RASPBERRY VINAIGRETTE (RECIPE
FOLLOWS)

Arrange the arugula on salad plates. Top each serving with the sliced pears and sprinkle
with the pecans. Drizzle with Raspberry Vinaigrette and serve at once.

RASPBERRY VINAIGRETTE

makes about 3 cups

---

2 CUPS FRESH OR FROZEN
RASPBERRIES

¼ CUP EXTRA-VIRGIN OLIVE OIL

¼ CUP AGAVE NECTAR

½ CUP PLUS 1 TABLESPOON RED WINE
VINEGAR

½ TEASPOON SEA SALT

½ CUP CHOPPED TOASTED PECANS
(SEE NOTE)

1. Put the raspberries, olive oil, agave nectar, vinegar, and salt in a blender and blend until
well combined. Strain through a fine sieve.

2. Add the pecans and blend again. The vinaigrette will keep in the refrigerator, covered, for
up to a week.

NOTE: To toast the pecans, spread them on a baking sheet and toast them in a
preheated 350°F oven or toaster oven for about 5 minutes, until golden brown. Shake the
pan once or twice for even toasting. Slide the nuts off the baking sheet to stop the cooking
and let them cool.

KALE AND RED PEPPER SLAW WITH SPICY CITRUS DRESSING

serves 4 to 6

Kale, a member of the cabbage family, is a wonderful addition to salads, soups, and stews. It is loaded with vitamins A and C, folic acid, calcium, and iron—and it's delicious. Here we use it in a salad with marinated and baked tofu and Spicy Citrus Dressing. Be sure to buy kale at its very freshest, store it in the refrigerator, and use it within five days.

1 BLOCK TOFU, CUT INTO SMALL CUBES

2 GARLIC CLOVES, MINCED

1 TABLESPOON FRESH GINGER, MINCED

½ TEASPOON CRUSHED RED PEPPER FLAKES

2 TABLESPOONS SESAME OIL

2 TABLESPOONS BROWN RICE VINEGAR

⅓ CUP SHOYU OR TAMARI SOY SAUCE

1 BUNCH KALE, CUT INTO BITE-SIZED PIECES

1 RED BELL PEPPER, SEEDED, DEVEINED, AND CUT INTO 1-INCH JULIENNE

1 CARROT, PEELED AND CUT INTO 1-INCH JULIENNE

1 BUNCH OF SCALLIONS, THINLY SLICED

2 TABLESPOONS SESAME SEEDS, TOASTED (SEE PAGE 160)

SPICY CITRUS DRESSING (RECIPE FOLLOWS)

1. Preheat the oven to 375°F.

2. Put the tofu in a baking dish. Put the garlic, ginger, and red pepper flakes in a bowl. Whisk in the sesame oil, vinegar, and shoyu or tamari soy sauce. Pour over the tofu and let sit for 45 minutes. Bake, uncovered, for 10 minutes, turn and cook for an additional 10 to 15 minutes, until the cubes begin to crisp. Remove the tofu with a slotted spoon and set aside to cool.

3. Blanch the kale in boiling water for 45 seconds. Remove and submerge in ice water. Drain and cool.

4. Toss together the kale, tofu, red bell pepper, carrot, scallion, and sesame seeds. Add the Spicy Citrus Dressing and toss again. Taste and adjust the seasonings and serve at once.

SPICY CITRUS DRESSING

makes about 1 cup

This fabulous dressing is not only great with Kale and Red Pepper Slaw but
also with grilled seitan and tempeh and over salad greens.

¼ CUP SHOYU OR TAMARI SOY SAUCE

¼ CUP BROWN RICE VINEGAR

JUICE OF 1 LIME

3 TABLESPOONS TOASTED SESAME OIL

1 TABLESPOON CHILI SAUCE, OR HOT
SAUCE

Mix the shoyu or tamari soy sauce, vinegar, and lime together in a bowl. Slowly add the
sesame oil, whisking constantly until smooth. Add the chili sauce and whisk again. The dressing will keep in the refrigerator, covered, for up to a week. Bring to room temperature and
whisk well before serving.

ROASTED VEGETABLE SALAD WITH ROASTED GARLIC DRESSING

serves 4

Abigael Birrell, a Candle chef, invented this luscious salad, full of roasted seasonal vegetables. She likes to serve it as a starter to a festive holiday dinner. It's also a good main-course salad.

1 FENNEL BULB, TRIMMED AND CUT INTO BITE-SIZED PIECES

2 MEDIUM RED BELL PEPPERS, SEEDED, DEVEINED, AND CUT INTO THIN STRIPS

½ POUND FINGERLING OR NEW POTATOES, CUT INTO BITE-SIZED PIECES (ABOUT 2 CUPS)

¼ POUND BABY TURNIPS, PEELED AND CUT INTO BITE-SIZED PIECES (ABOUT 1 CUP)

2 MEDIUM BEETS, PEELED AND CUT INTO BITE-SIZED PIECES

1 TABLESPOON SEA SALT FRESHLY GROUND BLACK PEPPER

5 TABLESPOONS EXTRA-VIRGIN OLIVE OIL ROASTED GARLIC DRESSING (RECIPE FOLLOWS)

2 BUNCHES OF ARUGULA, RINSED, TRIMMED, AND STEMMED

½ CUP TOASTED PECANS OR WALNUTS (OPTIONAL; SEE NOTE, PAGE 75)

¼ CUP DRIED CURRANTS OR CRANBERRIES (OPTIONAL)

1. Preheat the oven to 400°F.

2. In a large mixing bowl, toss the vegetables with the salt, pepper to taste, and olive oil. Spread in a single layer on a baking sheet and bake until just tender, 35 to 40 minutes. Toss the vegetables with about 2 tablespoons of Roasted Garlic Dressing to lightly coat the vegetables and set aside.

3. To serve the salad, arrange the arugula, evenly divided, on 4 plates, then top with equal amounts of the warm vegetable mixture. Sprinkle with toasted walnuts or pecans and currants or cranberries, if desired. Drizzle with a bit more dressing and serve at once.

ROASTED GARLIC DRESSING

makes 2 cups

We always keep a good amount of Roasted Garlic Dressing on hand.
Not only is it excellent on salads, but we also serve it with roasted
or steamed vegetables, rice, and grains.

1 CUP PEELED GARLIC CLOVES

1 CUP EXTRA-VIRGIN OLIVE OIL

¼ CUP BALSAMIC VINEGAR

¼ CUP SHERRY WINE VINEGAR OR RED WINE VINEGAR

1 TABLESPOON WHITE MISO

2 TABLESPOONS MINCED FRESH THYME OR 1 TEASPOON DRIED OREGANO

PINCH OF GRATED NUTMEG

1 TEASPOON SEA SALT

2 TEASPOONS FRESHLY GROUND BLACK PEPPER

1. Preheat the oven to 350°F.

2. Put the peeled garlic cloves in a baking dish and cover with the olive oil. Cover the dish with foil and roast approximately 25 minutes, or until golden brown. When cool enough to handle, remove the garlic with a slotted spoon and transfer to a blender. Reserve the roasted garlic oil for another use (see Note).

3. Add ½ cup water, the vinegars, miso, thyme or oregano, nutmeg, salt, and pepper and blend until smooth. Add a bit more water if necessary. The dressing will keep in the refrigerator, covered, for up to a week.

NOTE: The reserved roasted garlic oil will keep in a covered container for up to a week. Use it to drizzle over pasta, vegetables, and salad greens. It's also excellent when used in sautés and stir-fries.

AZTEC SALAD

serves 4

One of our chefs, Jonathan Grumbles, designed this recipe as a balanced meal that's full of the flavors of Mexico. All of the components can be prepared well ahead of time and tossed together just before serving.

TEMPEH

- 8 OUNCES TEMPEH, QUARTERED
- 1 CUP APPLE JUICE
- 1 CUP SHOYU OR TAMARI SOY SAUCE
- ¼ CUP PEELED AND SHREDDED FRESH GINGER
- 2 GARLIC CLOVES, MINCED
- 1 CUP AGAVE NECTAR
- CHIPOTLE BARBECUE SAUCE (RECIPE FOLLOWS)

QUINOA SALAD

- 1½ CUPS QUINOA
- 1 TABLESPOON SEA SALT
- 2 EARS OF SWEET CORN, HUSKED
- 1 RED ONION, PEELED AND THINLY SLICED
- 1 CUP CHOPPED CILANTRO

- 1 RED BELL PEPPER, SEEDED, DEVEINED, AND CUT INTO THIN STRIPS
- 1 CUP BLACK BEANS, COOKED AND DRAINED, OR 2 CUPS DRAINED AND RINSED CANNED BEANS
- JUICE OF 1 LIME
- ROASTED TOMATO VINAIGRETTE (PAGE 82)

TOASTED PUMPKIN SEEDS

- 1 CUP RAW UNSALTED PUMPKIN SEEDS
- 2 TEASPOONS EXTRA-VIRGIN OLIVE OIL
- 1 TEASPOON SEA SALT
- ½ TEASPOON CHILI POWDER

- 4 CUPS MESCLUN

1. Preheat the oven to 350°F.

2. To prepare the tempeh, place the tempeh quarters in a single layer in a baking dish. In a medium bowl, mix together the apple juice, shoyu or tamari soy sauce, ⅔ cup of water, the ginger, garlic, and agave nectar and pour over the tempeh. Cover and bake for 45 minutes. Drain the tempeh and let it cool.

3. Prepare a stovetop or charcoal grill or heat up the broiler. Brush the tempeh with the Chipotle Barbecue Sauce and grill until lightly browned, about 3 minutes per side.

4. To prepare the quinoa salad, rinse the quinoa until the water runs clear, then drain. In a medium saucepan, bring 2¾ cups of water and the salt to a boil. Add the quinoa, reduce the heat, and simmer. Cover and cook for 20 to 25 minutes. Fluff with a fork and remove the quinoa to a large bowl. Fluff again and set aside to cool.

5. In a medium saucepan, cook the corn in boiling salted water for 8 minutes. Drain and cool. Scrape the kernels off the ears with a sharp knife and set aside.

6. In a large bowl, toss the onion, cilantro, red pepper, and black beans together. Add the lime juice and toss again. Mix into the quinoa and gently toss together. Add about ¼ cup Roasted Tomato Vinaigrette and toss again.

7. Preheat the oven to 375°F.

8. To prepare the Toasted Pumpkin Seeds, toss the pumpkin seeds with the olive oil, salt, and chili powder in a small bowl. Spread on a baking sheet and bake until the seeds just begin to pop, 5 to 7 minutes. Set aside to cool.

9. To assemble the salad, divide the mesclun among 4 salad bowls. Place about 1 cup of the dressed quinoa mixture on top of the lettuce. Slice each tempeh square into triangles and place 4 triangles of tempeh over the quinoa in a spoke pattern. Sprinkle with the pumpkin seeds and drizzle with a small amount of vinaigrette.

CHIPOTLE BARBECUE SAUCE

makes 5 cups

This spicy sauce is a great pantry item. It's great to have some on hand to use over grilled tofu or seitan. It's also delicious with grilled vegetables.

3 DRIED CHIPOTLE PEPPERS

3 TABLESPOONS MINCED GARLIC

1½ CUPS TOMATO PASTE

1 CUP APPLE CIDER VINEGAR

½ CUP MOLASSES

1 CUP AGAVE NECTAR

¼ CUP DIJON MUSTARD

¾ CUP DRIED BASIL

1 TEASPOON SEA SALT

FRESHLY GROUND BLACK PEPPER

½ CUP SHOYU OR TAMARI SOY SAUCE

1. Soak the peppers in hot water to cover for 15 minutes. Drain and chop.

2. Place the chopped chipotles and the remaining ingredients with 1 cup of water in a blender and blend until smooth. The sauce will keep, covered, in the refrigerator for up to 2 weeks.

ROASTED TOMATO VINAIGRETTE

makes 3 cups

This is a versatile and delicious dressing. Its robust flavor holds up to a
variety of vegetables and grains, as well as salads.

---

4 PLUM TOMATOES, HALVED

1¼ CUPS PLUS 1 TABLESPOON
EXTRA-VIRGIN OLIVE OIL

½ TEASPOON SEA SALT

FRESHLY GROUND BLACK PEPPER

½ CUP RED WINE VINEGAR

1 TEASPOON CRUSHED RED PEPPER
FLAKES

2 GARLIC CLOVES, MINCED

2 TABLESPOONS CHOPPED CILANTRO

1. Preheat the oven to 400°F.

2. Toss the tomatoes with 1 tablespoon of the olive oil, the salt, and pepper to taste. Place
the tomatoes on a baking sheet, cut-side down, and roast for 20 to 25 minutes, until the skin
blisters. Set aside to cool.

3. Transfer to a blender the tomatoes, the remaining 1¼ cups olive oil, vinegar, red pepper
flakes, garlic, cilantro, and salt and pepper to taste; blend until smooth. Taste and adjust the
seasonings. The vinaigrette will keep, covered, in the refrigerator for up to a week.

VARIATION: For a Spicy Southwestern-Style Roasted Tomato Vinaigrette, add
4 rehydrated chipotles to the tomatoes before blending.

TOASTED MILLET SALAD WITH CURRY-MISO VINAIGRETTE

serves 6 to 8

Millet, which is not a widely used grain, is a nutritionally powerful food. It is higher in protein content than wheat and surpasses whole wheat and brown rice in B vitamins, copper, and iron. In addition to being easy to digest, it is gluten-free and very rich in amino acids and phosphorus. Its delicate, nutty flavor is the highlight of this salad.

3 CUPS MILLET, RINSED

SEA SALT

1 CUP DRIED CHICKPEAS, COOKED AND DRAINED, OR 1 CUP CANNED CHICKPEAS, RINSED AND DRAINED

1 CUP SHREDDED CARROTS

2 MEDIUM RED BELL PEPPERS, SEEDED, DEVEINED, AND THINLY SLICED

CURRY-MISO VINAIGRETTE (RECIPE FOLLOWS)

6 CUPS MESCLUN

1. Heat a heavy-bottomed soup pot over medium heat and toast the millet, stirring constantly, for 1 to 2 minutes, until the millet just begins to brown and give off a nutty aroma. Add 6 cups of water and salt to taste and bring to a boil. Reduce the heat, cover, and simmer for about 30 minutes. Drain and spread the millet on a baking sheet to cool.

2. Put the cooled millet in a large bowl and add the chickpeas, carrots, and peppers. Toss with 1¼ cups of Curry-Miso Vinaigrette.

3. Toss the mesclun with the remaining vinaigrette and divide among 6 to 8 plates. Top each serving with the millet mixture and serve at once.

CURRY-MISO VINAIGRETTE

makes 2 cups

This tasty vinaigrette is a good accompaniment to a variety of vegetables, rice, and grains.

½ CUP BROWN RICE VINEGAR

1¼ CUPS SAFFLOWER OIL

¼ CUP MELLOW WHITE MISO

1 TABLESPOON CURRY POWDER

1 TEASPOON GRATED FRESH GINGER

1 GARLIC CLOVE, MINCED

1 TABLESPOON AGAVE NECTAR

Place all of the ingredients with ¼ cup of water in a blender and blend until well incorporated. The vinaigrette will keep in the refrigerator, covered, for up to a week.

SEA SALAD WITH MISO-MIRIN DRESSING

serves 6

Seaweed is rich in important nutrients and minerals. It is especially good for
maintaining healthy skin and hair. We make this Asian-style salad with
two types of seaweed and plenty of vegetables for a great texture.

½ CUP SHOYU OR TAMARI SOY SAUCE

1 TABLESPOON SESAME OIL

1 TABLESPOON FINELY SHREDDED
FRESH GINGER

2 GARLIC CLOVES, MINCED

¼ CUP BROWN RICE VINEGAR

2 TABLESPOONS UMEBOSHI VINEGAR

1 POUND FIRM TOFU, CUT LENGTHWISE
INTO 3 PIECES

½ CUP DRIED ARAME

½ CUP DRIED HIZIKI

⅓ CUP FINELY SHREDDED RED
CABBAGE

⅓ CUP FINELY SHREDDED GREEN
CABBAGE

1 RED BELL PEPPER, SEEDED,
DEVEINED, AND CUT INTO 1-INCH
STRIPS

2 CARROTS, PEELED AND FINELY
SHREDDED

5 SCALLIONS, FINELY CHOPPED

MISO-MIRIN DRESSING (RECIPE
FOLLOWS)

5 CUPS MESCLUN

½ CUP FRESH PEA SHOOTS, FOR
GARNISH (OPTIONAL)

1. In a small bowl, whisk ½ cup of water, the shoyu or tamari soy sauce, sesame oil, ginger,
garlic, and vinegars together. Place the tofu in a baking dish and pour the marinade over it.
Let stand for at least 30 minutes. Grill the tofu over a charcoal or stovetop grill, or broil
until browned, about 4 minutes per side. Set aside to cool.

2. Place the arame and hiziki in separate bowls with hot water just to cover and soak for
5 minutes. Drain and set aside.

3. In a medium bowl, toss the cabbages, red bell pepper, carrots, scallions, arame, and hiziki
together with a tablespoon of the dressing.

4. To serve the salad, divide the mesclun among 6 salad plates and top with the vegetable
and seaweed mixture. Cut the grilled tofu into triangles and place over it. Garnish with the
pea shoots, if using, and drizzle with a bit more dressing.

MISO-MIRIN DRESSING

makes 1 ½ cups

Sweet and salty Miso-Mirin Dressing, which resembles a Japanese dipping sauce, is a wonderful complement to Sea Salad. We serve it with stir-fries, soba noodles, and brown rice. It keeps very well in the refrigerator for up to 2 weeks.

¼ CUP MIRIN

¼ CUP SHOYU OR TAMARI SOY SAUCE

¼ CUP BROWN RICE VINEGAR

¼ CUP MISO

Place ½ cup of water, the mirin, shoyu or tamari soy sauce, vinegar, and miso in a blender and blend until well incorporated.

SPICY SOBA SALAD WITH CREAMY WASABI DRESSING

serves 4

This delicious combination of cooked tofu, soba noodles, and arame tossed
with Creamy Wasabi Dressing and served over a bed of mixed
Asian greens is a nutritious meal in itself.

TOFU

- ¼ CUP SHOYU OR TAMARI SOY SAUCE
- 2 TEASPOONS SESAME OIL
- 2 TEASPOONS SHREDDED FRESH GINGER
- 2 GARLIC CLOVES, MINCED
- 2 TABLESPOONS BROWN RICE VINEGAR
- 2 TABLESPOONS UMEBOSHI VINEGAR
- 1 POUND FIRM TOFU, CUT INTO 4 PIECES

ARAME

- 1 CUP ARAME
- 2 TEASPOONS BROWN RICE VINEGAR
- ½ TEASPOON MIRIN
- ¼ TEASPOON TOASTED SESAME OIL
- 2 TEASPOONS AGAVE NECTAR
- 2 CUPS MIXED ASIAN GREENS, SUCH AS MIZUNA, TATSOI, OR BABY BOK CHOY
- 1 POUND SOBA NOODLES, COOKED AND DRAINED
- 1 CUP SNOW PEA SHOOTS
- ½ CUP FINELY SHREDDED CARROTS
  CREAMY WASABI DRESSING (RECIPE FOLLOWS)

1. In a small bowl, whisk together ¼ cup of water, the shoyu or tamari soy sauce, oil, ginger, garlic, and vinegars. Place the tofu in a baking dish and pour the mixture over them. Marinate in the refrigerator for at least 3 hours or up to overnight.

2. Preheat the oven to 350°F.

3. Bake the tofu for 15 to 20 minutes and set aside to cool. Cut into triangles.

4. Meanwhile, soak the arame in 1 cup of boiling water for 5 minutes, until tender. Drain and rinse. Whisk together the vinegar, mirin, toasted sesame oil, and agave nectar. Toss together with the arame.

5. Divide the greens among 4 plates. Toss the cooked soba noodles with the arame, then place over the greens. Top each serving with an equal amount of tofu triangles and garnish with the snow pea shoots and carrots. Drizzle with Creamy Wasabi Dressing.

CRYSTAL ROLLS (PAGE 22) AND NORI ROLLS (PAGE 23)

MINI POTATO LATKES (PAGE 10) WITH TOFU-CILANTRO SOUR CREAM (PAGE 167) AND
EGGPLANT-HIZIKI CAVIAR (PAGE 11)

TOP: CANDLE CAFE'S MEZZE PLATTER (PAGES 14-17)
BOTTOM: TOFU SATAY WITH COCONUT PEANUT SAUCE (PAGE 18) AND SEITAN
SKEWERS WITH CHIMICHURRI CITRUS-HERB SAUCE (PAGE 20)

GRILLED VEGETABLE NAPOLEON (PAGE 9)

VELVETY CARROT AND GINGER SOUP (PAGE 50) WITH BLUE CORN QUINOA CORN BREAD (PAGE 151)

TOP: SHIITAKE AND SCALLION BROTH (PAGE 40)
BOTTOM: SPRING VEGETABLE MINESTRONE (PAGE 44)

TOP: CANDLE COBB SALAD WITH CARROT-GINGER DRESSING (PAGE 68)
BOTTOM: ASPARAGUS, ALMOND, AND TOMATO SALAD WITH
MUSTARD-DILL VINAIGRETTE (PAGE 89)

ROASTED VEGETABLE SALAD WITH ROASTED GARLIC DRESSING (PAGE 78)

BARBECUED TEMPEH-CHIPOTLE BURGER WITH GRILLED PINEAPPLE (PAGE 102),
MANGO KETCHUP (PAGE 158), AND LEMON CARAWAY SLAW (PAGE 139)

TOP: MARINATED GRILLED TOFU (PAGE 153), ROASTED ROOTS (PAGE 143),
AND MAPLE-CINNAMON SQUASH RINGLETS (PAGE 142)
BOTTOM: CORNMEAL-CRUSTED TEMPEH (PAGE 121) WITH SAUTEED MIXED GREENS
(PAGE 147), BARBECUED BEANS (PAGE 152), AND SWEET POTATO SMASH (PAGE 144)

TEX-MEX TOSTADAS (PAGE 126)

INDIAN WRAPS (PAGE 104), MEXICAN WRAPS (PAGE 106),
AND MIDDLE EASTERN WRAPS (PAGE 107)

SEITAN PICCATA WITH WHITE WINE AND CAPER SAUCE (PAGE 119),
WITH GRILLED ASPARAGUS AND OYSTER MUSHROOMS

TOP: CINNAMON CRUMB COFFEE CAKE (PAGE 200)
BOTTOM: TOFU SCRAMBLE WITH YUKON GOLD AND
SWEET POTATO HOME FRIES (PAGE 204)

TOP: BLACK AND WHITE CUPCAKES (PAGE 178)
BOTTOM: APPLE PIE (PAGE 179)

TOP: VANILLA-SCENTED POACHED PEARS (PAGE 195) AND
CHOCOLATE MACADAMIA NUT COOKIES (PAGE 191)
BOTTOM: LEMON TOFU CHEESECAKE WITH BLOOD ORANGE GLAZE (PAGE 174)

CREAMY WASABI DRESSING

makes 3 cups

Here is a great salad dressing and excellent sushi dip loaded
with good flavor and a spicy kick.

⅓ CUP WASABI POWDER

1 CUP SESAME TAHINI

⅓ CUP BROWN RICE VINEGAR

⅓ CUP SHOYU OR TAMARI SOY SAUCE

In a small bowl, dissolve the wasabi powder in 2 cups of water. Transfer to a blender, add
the tahini, vinegar, and shoyu or tamari soy sauce, and blend until smooth. The dressing will
keep, covered, in the refrigerator for up to 2 weeks.

MIXED SPROUT SALAD WITH VANILLA-TAHINI DRESSING

serves 6

Try this easy, healthy salad topped with Vanilla-Tahini Dressing for a light lunch.
We like to mix a variety of sprouts together and enjoy their crunchy, nutty texture.
You will, too.

6 CUPS MESCLUN

16 OUNCES MIXED SPROUTS, SUCH AS
SNOW PEA, ALFALFA, AND/OR
BUCKWHEAT SPROUTS (SEE NOTE)

6 OUNCES SNOW PEA SHOOTS

4 OUNCES ALFALFA SPROUTS

1 CUP SHREDDED CARROTS

VANILLA-TAHINI DRESSING (RECIPE
FOLLOWS)

½ CUP RAISINS, FOR GARNISH

2 TABLESPOONS SESAME SEEDS, FOR
GARNISH

Divide the greens among 6 plates. Top with the crunchy sprouts, snow pea shoots, buckwheat sprouts, then the alfalfa sprouts. Top each salad with the carrots and drizzle with
Vanilla-Tahini Dressing. Garnish with the raisins and sesame seeds and serve at once.

NOTE: Crunchy sprouts are available in health food stores. We use The Sproutman
brand, which includes a combination of organic adzuki bean, lentil, and chickpea sprouts.

VANILLA-TAHINI DRESSING

makes 4 cups

A hint of vanilla adds an interesting and unique flavor to this sesame-flavored
dressing. It is also excellent served over warm rice or grains.

2 CUPS TAHINI

2 GARLIC CLOVES, MINCED

3 TABLESPOONS FRESH LEMON JUICE

1 TEASPOON VANILLA EXTRACT

1 TABLESPOON SHOYU OR TAMARI SOY
SAUCE (OR A PINCH OF SEA SALT)

Put all of the ingredients with 2 cups of water in a blender or bowl and blend or whisk
together until very smooth. Add more water if the dressing seems too thick. The dressing
will keep in the refrigerator, covered, for up to 3 days. Bring to room temperature
before using.

ASPARAGUS, ALMOND, AND TOMATO SALAD WITH MUSTARD-DILL VINAIGRETTE

serves 6

This salad with garden-fresh asparagus and cherry tomatoes is a very refreshing starter. We also like to use the vinaigrette as a dip for raw vegetables and pita crisps.

2½ TO 3 POUNDS SLENDER FRESH ASPARAGUS

6 CUPS FRESH SALAD GREENS, SUCH AS MESCLUN MIX, RED LEAF LETTUCE, BOSTON LETTUCE, BIBB LETTUCE, OR GREEN LEAF LETTUCE

1 CUP CHERRY TOMATOES, HALVED

MUSTARD-DILL VINAIGRETTE (RECIPE FOLLOWS)

¼ CUP SLICED ALMONDS

1. Cut or break off the tough woody ends of the asparagus stalks and discard.

2. In a large saucepan or skillet, bring enough lightly salted water to cover the asparagus to a boil over high heat. Add the asparagus, reduce the heat to a simmer, and cook for 3 to 5 minutes, just until tender. Drain well. Chill the asparagus for an hour.

3. Toss the greens and tomatoes together with about ⅓ cup of the vinaigrette. Toss the asparagus in a separate bowl with about 2 tablespoons of the vinaigrette, then place over the salad greens. Sprinkle with the almonds and add a bit more vinaigrette, if desired. Serve at once.

MUSTARD-DILL VINAIGRETTE

makes 2 cups

1 CUP SAFFLOWER OIL

4 GARLIC CLOVES, SLICED

¼ CUP FRESH DILL

2 TABLESPOONS DIJON MUSTARD

½ CUP RED WINE VINEGAR

¼ CUP WATER

Place all the ingredients in a blender or food processor fitted with a steel blade and blend until smooth. The vinaigrette will keep, covered, in the refrigerator for up to 2 weeks.

SANDWICHES, BURGERS, AND WRAPS

We love to create all types of healthy sandwiches, burgers, and wraps at the Candle. Many of our customers pop into the restaurant for a Tofu Club Sandwich, a Black Bean Burger, or one of our many international wraps.

All of our sandwiches and wraps are made of very fresh and healthful ingredients. Fresh tofu, seitan, or tempeh and beans, grains, and fresh vegetables fill our sandwiches and wraps. Burgers are made with brown rice, a variety of lentils, soy cheese, and portobello mushrooms and are just delicious.

TOFU CLUB SANDWICHES ON MULTI-GRAIN TOAST

makes 2 sandwiches

Our tofu club sandwich is a delicious and healthy twist on the classic version.
It's a mainstay of our lunch menu and we serve many of them every day at the Candle.
Keep all the components on hand in your refrigerator and you can assemble
the sandwich as soon as you crave it. Pickles, coleslaw, and homemade
potato chips make ideal accompaniments.

4 SLICES OF MULTI-GRAIN BREAD

2 TABLESPOONS VEGAN MAYO
(PAGE 166)

2 SLICES OF MARINATED GRILLED TOFU
(PAGE 153)

4 SLICES OF RIPE TOMATO

4 SLICES OF TEMPEH BACON, COOKED
AND DRAINED

4 ROMAINE LETTUCE LEAVES, TRIMMED

For each sandwich, toast the multi-grain bread, then spread a tablespoon of Vegan Mayo
over the toast. Place a slice of grilled tofu on it, then top with 2 slices each of tomato and
tempeh bacon and 2 lettuce leaves. Cover with another slice of bread, place toothpicks
through the sandwich, then slice into 4 triangles.

VARIATIONS: Some of our regulars claim the Tofu Club is best with Russian Dressing
(page 95)—others love it with Carrot-Ginger Dressing (page 69) or Creamy Chipotle Ranch Dressing
(page 71).

TUSCAN WHITE BEAN PÂ
SANDWICHES WITH ARUG
AND TOMATO

makes 4 sandwiches

This hearty and delicious sandwich is always a smash hit. We usually make it with a crusty French baguette, but it's also delicious with pumpernickel or rye bread.

WHITE BEAN PÂTÉ

2 CUPS COOKED WHITE BEANS (SEE CHART, PAGE 211)

1 TEASPOON SESAME TAHINI

2 SMALL GARLIC CLOVES

2 WHOLE DATES, PITTED AND CHOPPED

2 TEASPOONS FRESH LEMON JUICE

1 TEASPOON UMEBOSHI VINEGAR

1 BAGUETTE

1 CUP ARUGULA LEAVES, RINSED AND COARSELY CHOPPED

2 MEDIUM TOMATOES, THINLY SLICED

1. Place the beans, tahini, garlic, dates, lemon juice, vinegar, and ⅓ cup of water in a blender or food processor and blend until smooth. The pâté will keep in the refrigerator, covered, for up to 5 days.

2. To assemble sandwiches, slice the baguette horizontally and spread with the bean pâté. Top with the arugula and tomato slices and cut into 4 sandwiches.

GRILLED SEITAN STEAK HEROES

makes 2 sandwiches

Grilled seitan takes on a wonderfully rich flavor, especially when it's marinated or basted with a flavorful vinaigrette. Try this juicy hero sandwich with homemade ketchup, Russian Dressing (page 95), or mustard—it's all good.

8 OUNCES SEITAN, CUT INTO ½-INCH SLICES

¼ CUP UNIVERSAL MARINADE (PAGE 164)

2 HERO ROLLS

¼ CUP CARAMELIZED ONIONS (PAGE 147)

4 ROMAINE LETTUCE LEAVES

1. Prepare a gas, charcoal, or stovetop grill. Grill the seitan slices, about 4 minutes a side, basting each side with the marinade. The seitan can also be prepared in a broiler.

2. Split the hero rolls and place the grilled seitan slices on them. Top with the caramelized onions and lettuce. Serve with assorted condiments.

SOUTHWESTERN-STYLE CHILE-RUBBED SEITAN SANDWICHES

makes 3 sandwiches

We make this spicy sandwich with guajillo peppers, which are very flavorful.
They are found in good produce markets and specialty stores.
Enjoy these sandwiches with cold Mexican beer.

---

4 DRIED GUAJILLO OR 2 DRIED CHIPOTLE PEPPERS, SEEDED

1 TEASPOON SEA SALT

1 TABLESPOON APPLE CIDER VINEGAR

1 TEASPOON GROUND CUMIN

1 GARLIC CLOVE, PEELED AND CHOPPED

PINCH OF DRIED THYME

PINCH OF DRIED OREGANO

1 POUND SEITAN, CUT INTO ½-INCH SLICES

¼ CUP EXTRA-VIRGIN OLIVE OIL

½ CUP CARAMELIZED ONIONS (PAGE 147)

3 SLICES OF RIPE TOMATO

6 SLICES OF MULTI-GRAIN BREAD

CHIPOTLE MAYO (PAGE 166)

1. Preheat the oven to 350°F.

2. Place the peppers on a baking sheet and bake until oven-dried, about 10 to 15 minutes. When cool enough to handle, crush them with your hands or a rolling pin.

3. Place the peppers, salt, vinegar, a tablespoon of water, the cumin, garlic, thyme, and oregano in a food processor and blend thoroughly to make a paste. Rub the paste on the seitan slices and let sit for up to an hour or overnight.

4. Heat the olive oil in a skillet. Sauté the seitan slices, about 3 to 5 minutes per side. Remove the seitan slices from the pan with a slotted spoon and set aside.

5. To assemble each sandwich, layer a third of the seitan and caramelized onions and a slice of tomato on a slice of the bread. Top with a second slice of bread spread with chipotle mayonnaise.

TEMPEH REUBEN SANDWICHES

makes 4 sandwiches

We have updated and slimmed down the classic Reuben sandwich with marinated and cooked tempeh. It's delicious served with our version of homemade Russian Dressing.

1 CUP APPLE JUICE

2 TABLESPOONS MAPLE SYRUP OR AGAVE NECTAR

¼ CUP SHOYU OR TAMARI SOY SAUCE

4 GARLIC CLOVES, FINELY CHOPPED

4 SLICES OF FRESH GINGER

2 8-OUNCE PACKAGES TEMPEH, CUT IN HALF HORIZONTALLY, THEN CUT INTO 4 SQUARES PER PACKAGE

8 SLICES OF RYE BREAD

½ CUP SAUERKRAUT

1 CUP CARAMELIZED ONIONS (PAGE 147)

RUSSIAN DRESSING (RECIPE FOLLOWS)

1. Preheat the oven to 350°F or prepare a charcoal, gas, or stovetop grill.

2. In a small bowl, mix together the apple juice, maple syrup or agave nectar, shoyu or tamari soy sauce, garlic, and ginger. Place the tempeh in a baking dish, add the marinade, and let sit for 30 minutes.

3. Bake the tempeh for 30 minutes, or if using a grill, cook over medium-hot heat for 2 to 3 minutes a side, basting with the marinade.

4. To assemble each sandwich, place 2 squares of cooked tempeh on a slice of rye bread and top with sauerkraut and onions. Spread a tablespoon of Russian Dressing on the other slice of bread. Place on top of the sandwich and slice in half.

RUSSIAN DRESSING

makes 1 cup

½ CUP VEGAN MAYO (PAGE 166)

¼ CUP KETCHUP

¼ CUP STONE-GROUND MUSTARD

¼ CUP FINELY CHOPPED ONION

In a small bowl, mix together the Vegan Mayo, ketchup, mustard, and onion until well combined. Chill for at least an hour before serving. The dressing will keep, covered, in the refrigerator, for up to 3 days.

FRENCH DIP SANDWICHES

makes 4 sandwiches

These seitan sandwiches, served with a deeply savory mushroom-flavored dipping sauce, are divine.

¼ CUP DRIED PORCINI MUSHROOMS

½ POUND SEITAN, CUT INTO 8 VERY THIN SLICES

3 CUPS ROASTED VEGETABLE BROTH (PAGE 39)

1 TABLESPOON MINCED ONION

1 ½ TABLESPOONS SHOYU OR TAMARI SOY SAUCE

2 TABLESPOONS SOY MARGARINE

2 SMALL FRENCH OR ITALIAN BAGUETTES

1. Place the porcini mushrooms in a small bowl and cover with ½ cup of water. Soak until softened, about 30 minutes. Drain and reserve the soaking liquid. Thinly slice the mushrooms and return to the broth.

2. In a medium saucepan, place the seitan slices. Add the vegetable broth and reserved mushroom soaking liquid. Bring to a boil, reduce the heat, and simmer over medium heat until thoroughly heated, stirring occasionally.

3. Add the minced onion, shoyu or tamari soy sauce, and margarine and cook for an additional 2 to 3 minutes. Remove the seitan slices with a slotted spoon and reserve the broth.

4. Cut each baguette in half horizontally, then split them lengthwise. Top 4 of the split baguettes with 2 slices of cooked seitan. Cover with the remaining 4 baguette pieces. Divide the hot broth into 4 individual serving cups and use for a dipping sauce.

VARIATION: For the old-fashioned Balboa Sandwich, toast the baguette slices and rub them with garlic. Top with seitan and melted soy cheese.

EGGPLANT PARMESAN SANDWICHES

makes 4 sandwiches

Here's a nice twist on classic eggplant Parmesan. We top breaded and cooked eggplant with homemade marinara sauce and soy cheese. We often double the recipe so that we can cut the sandwiches into bite-sized pieces to serve at parties.

½ CUP SOY MILK

1 TEASPOON ARROWROOT POWDER

1 TEASPOON DIJON MUSTARD

1 TEASPOON DRIED BASIL

1 TEASPOON DRIED OREGANO

1 TEASPOON DRIED THYME

SALT

1 CUP BREAD CRUMBS, PREFERABLY HOMEMADE (SEE PAGE 21)

1 LARGE EGGPLANT, PEELED AND CUT INTO ¼-INCH-THICK SLICES

2 TABLESPOONS EXTRA-VIRGIN OLIVE OIL

4 HERO ROLLS, HALVED LENGTHWISE

½ TO 1 CUP MARINARA SAUCE (PAGE 163)

4 SLICES OF SOY CHEESE

1. In a large bowl, whisk together the soy milk and arrowroot until the arrowroot is fully dissolved. Add the mustard, basil, oregano, thyme, and salt to taste to create a slurry for breading the eggplant.

2. Place the bread crumbs on a plate. Dredge the eggplant in the slurry mixture, shake off the excess, then dredge in the bread crumbs to coat evenly.

3. In a large skillet over medium heat, heat the oil and fry the eggplant slices in a single layer in the pan. Continue frying until both sides are golden brown, about 5 to 8 minutes. Drain on a plate lined with paper towels. If you'd rather bake the eggplant, place the breaded eggplant slices on a lightly oiled baking sheet. Bake in a preheated 400°F oven for 15 to 20 minutes, or until the eggplant is crisp on the outside and fork-tender inside.

4. To assemble each sandwich, place eggplant slices on the bottom half of the hero roll. Top with Marinara Sauce and one slice of soy cheese. Toast or broil briefly to melt the cheese, then top with the remaining hero roll half and eat right away.

ITALIANO ROLLERS

makes 2 rollers

always like to have fun with food, and making rollers is just that. They are
versatile—great for packing into picnic lunches and taking in the car
for impromptu road trips. We also like to cut them into smaller pieces,
or pinwheels, for quick and healthy snacks. We have invented many versions
of rollers, and this is one of our favorites.

¼ CUP SUN-DRIED TOMATOES (NOT THE ONES PACKED IN OIL)

2 LARGE WHOLE WHEAT TORTILLAS

2 TABLESPOONS DIJON MUSTARD

3 SLICES OF MOZZARELLA SOY CHEESE

3 SLICES OF GRILLED OR SAUTÉED TEMPEH BACON

6 WHOLE BASIL LEAVES, THINLY SLICED

4 ROMAINE LETTUCE LEAVES

1. Place the sun-dried tomatoes in a small bowl and add hot water just to cover. Soak until softened, about 10 minutes. Drain and set aside.

2. Lay out the tortillas and spread evenly with the mustard. Place 1½ slices each of cheese and bacon on each tortilla, then press the sun-dried tomatoes into the cheese. Sprinkle with the sliced basil and top with the lettuce leaves. Roll up the tortilla and seal with a dab of mustard if it starts to unravel. Serve whole or cut into pinwheels.

VARIATIONS: Here are some more great fillings:

- Hummus (page 14) and Watercress with Carrot-Ginger Dressing (page 69)
- Marinated Grilled Tofu (page 153) and vegetables
- Seitan strips with Caramelized Onions (page 147) and fresh baby spinach
- Tempeh bacon, lettuce, and tomato with Vegan Mayo (page 166)
- Nut butter with jelly and banana slices

PORTOBELLO MUSHROOM PANINI

makes 2 sandwiches

The portobello panini, a remake of an old Candle favorite, is a
combination of roasted portobello mushrooms, red peppers,
and arugula on ciabatta bread.

---

2 TABLESPOONS EXTRA-VIRGIN
OLIVE OIL

2 TABLESPOONS BALSAMIC VINEGAR

2 TEASPOONS SEA SALT

2 LARGE PORTOBELLO MUSHROOMS,
CUT INTO ¼-INCH SLICES

1 RED BELL PEPPER

1 LOAF OF CIABATTA BREAD, HALVED
AND SPLIT LENGTHWISE

4 TABLESPOONS HERB FARM DIP
(PAGE 30) OR HERBED TOFU SPREAD
(PAGE 32)

12 ARUGULA LEAVES

1. Preheat the oven to 300°F.

2. In a small bowl, combine 1 tablespoon of the olive oil with the vinegar and salt. Place the
mushroom slices on a baking sheet and brush with the mixture. Roast until the mushrooms are
fork-tender, about 20 minutes.

3. Brush the red pepper with the remaining tablespoon of olive oil. Hold the pepper with a
long fork over an open flame or roast under the broiler, turning often, until the skin gets
black on all sides. This will take about 7 to 10 minutes over the flame and about 10 to
15 minutes in the broiler. Put the pepper in a paper bag and close tightly to steam it. When
the pepper is cool enough to handle, peel off the skin and remove the seeds and stem.
Slice the pepper into strips.

4. To assemble the sandwiches, spread the ciabatta halves with Herb Farm Dip or Herbed Tofu
Spread. Layer with the arugula leaves and red pepper slices, and top with the portobello
slices to cover the length of the sandwiches. Spread the remainder of the dip on the other
sides of the bread and serve immediately.

ROWN RICE AND LENTIL BURGERS

makes 6 to 8 burgers

burger recipe, made with brown rice and lentils, can also be made into a
loaf and served warm with mashed potatoes and Wild Mushroom Gravy (page 165).
Served as burgers, they are also very good cold, topped with homemade ketchup
or any variation of Vegan Mayo (page 166).

½ CUP FRENCH LENTILS, RINSED AND
DRAINED

1 CUP BROWN RICE

2 TABLESPOONS EXTRA-VIRGIN
OLIVE OIL

2 GARLIC CLOVES, CHOPPED

1 MEDIUM RED ONION, CHOPPED

2 RED BELL PEPPERS, SEEDED,
DEVEINED, AND DICED

1 TEASPOON SEA SALT

1 TEASPOON CHIPOTLE PEPPER
POWDER OR CHILI POWDER

BREAD CRUMBS OR UNBLEACHED
WHITE FLOUR (OPTIONAL)

1. In a medium saucepan, bring 1½ cups of water to a boil. Add the lentils, reduce the heat,
   and cook until softened, about 15 minutes. Drain and set aside.

2. Meanwhile, in another medium saucepan, bring 2 cups of water to a boil, add the rice,
   reduce the heat, cover, and simmer until the rice is just tender, about 40 minutes. Drain and
   set aside.

3. In a sauté pan, heat the olive oil over medium heat and sauté the garlic, onion, and peppers
   until lightly browned.

4. Preheat the oven to 350°F.

5. In a large bowl, combine the lentils, rice, and vegetables. Add the salt and chipotle pepper
   powder and mix well. Add a bit of bread crumbs or flour to hold the mixture together, if
   needed. Make into burger-sized patties and place on a baking sheet, or press into a loaf
   pan. Bake burgers until slightly firm, about 15 minutes, or bake the loaf for about 25 minutes.

BLACK BEAN BURGERS

makes 8 burgers

These burgers are terrific when served on a whole wheat bun with fresh tom⟩
lettuce, and Mango Ketchup (page 158).

4 CUPS BLACK BEANS

1 CUP PEELED AND DICED CARROTS

1 CUP PEELED AND DICED ONION

¾ CUP DICED RED BELL PEPPER

¾ CUP DICED GREEN OR YELLOW BELL
PEPPER

½ TEASPOON SEA SALT

½ CUP PLUS 1 TEASPOON EXTRA-VIRGIN
OLIVE OIL

¾ CUP CORNMEAL

½ TEASPOON GROUND CUMIN

2 TABLESPOONS CHILI POWDER

¼ TEASPOON CAYENNE

1 CUP CHICKPEA FLOUR

1½ TEASPOONS FRESH LEMON JUICE

½ CUP CHOPPED CILANTRO

8 WHOLE WHEAT BUNS
SLICED TOMATOES, FOR GARNISH
LETTUCE, FOR GARNISH

1. In a large saucepan, simmer the beans in 5 cups of water for 35 minutes. Drain the beans, reserving 1 cup of the cooking liquid.

2. In a large bowl, mix together the carrots, onion, peppers, salt, 1 teaspoon olive oil, and cornmeal. Stir in the cumin, chili powder, cayenne, chickpea flour, lemon juice, and cilantro. Stir in the black beans and form into patties. Add a bit of the reserved cooking liquid to the mixture to moisten if it is too dry. Or if you prefer a smoother-textured burger, blend half of the mixture in a blender until smooth and combine with the remaining mixture.

3. In a skillet, heat the remaining ½ cup olive oil and cook the burgers for about 3 minutes on each side. Serve on whole wheat buns with a slice of tomato and lettuce.

ARBECUED TEMPEH-CHIPOTLE BURGERS WITH GRILLED PINEAPPLE

makes 6 burgers

This is an excellent entrée for a summer barbecue. The spicy burgers pair very nicely with Lemon-Caraway Slaw (page 139) and a wild rice salad.

———————◆———————

3 DRIED CHIPOTLE CHILES OR
  2 TEASPOONS CHILI POWDER

2 GARLIC CLOVES, MINCED

1½ CUPS TOMATO PASTE

1 CUP APPLE CIDER VINEGAR

½ CUP MOLASSES

1 CUP AGAVE NECTAR

¼ CUP DIJON MUSTARD

1 TEASPOON DRIED BASIL

1 TEASPOON SEA SALT
  FRESHLY GROUND BLACK PEPPER

1 8-OUNCE PACKAGE TEMPEH, CUT
  INTO 6 CIRCLES

6 ½-INCH PINEAPPLE ROUNDS

6 WHOLE WHEAT BUNS
  MANGO KETCHUP (PAGE 158)

1. Soak the chipotle chiles in hot water for 15 minutes. Drain and place in a blender with the garlic, tomato paste, vinegar, molasses, agave nectar, mustard, basil, salt, pepper to taste, and 1 cup of water and blend until smooth.

2. Place the tempeh squares in a bowl and pour the chipotle mixture over them. Cover tightly and let marinate in the refrigerator overnight.

3. Prepare a charcoal, gas, or stovetop grill. Remove the tempeh from the marinade with a slotted spoon. Grill the tempeh and the pineapple rounds over medium-high heat, about 4 to 5 minutes per side, basting the tempeh with the marinade.

4. Toast the buns and then place a grilled tempeh circle and pineapple round on each of them. Serve with Mango Ketchup.

PORTOBELLO MUSHROOM BURGERS

makes 4 burgers

Portobello burgers are a huge favorite of ours. We simply throw these hearty mushrooms on the grill along with fresh red peppers and sweet Vidalia onions. When they're grilled to perfection, we layer everything on a whole wheat bun, garnish with Mango Ketchup, and dig in!!!

---

4 LARGE PORTOBELLO MUSHROOMS, STEMMED

2 RED BELL PEPPERS, HALVED, SEEDED, AND DEVEINED

½ TO ¾ CUP HERBED VINAIGRETTE (PAGE 73)

1 LARGE VIDALIA ONION, CUT INTO 4 THICK SLICES

4 WHOLE WHEAT BUNS

1 RIPE TOMATO, CUT INTO 4 THICK SLICES

MANGO KETCHUP (PAGE 158), FOR GARNISH

1. Prepare a charcoal or gas grill. Grill the mushrooms and peppers over medium-hot heat, basting with the vinaigrette until softened, about 3 to 4 minutes per side. Add the onion slices, baste with the vinaigrette, and grill until softened, about 5 minutes a side. (Turn the onion slices carefully so that they don't fall apart.)

2. Lightly toast the buns, then layer with the grilled portobello, red peppers, onion, and tomato. Serve with Mango Ketchup or any other favorite condiment.

INTERNATIONAL WRAPS

We have always incorporated influences from all over the world in our food, and these hearty and nutritious wraps are no exception. Whether it's an Indian Wrap with a mélange of Indian spices, black-eyed peas, and sautéed greens; a Mexican Wrap with chipotle and jalapeño peppers, avocados, and black beans; or a Middle Eastern Wrap with smoky grilled eggplant, chickpeas, and couscous, they never fail to satisfy.

The beans and grains are prepared ahead of time, and the other components are put together right before assembling them. If you make most of the elements in advance, assembling the wraps is a snap and you can whip up lunch in no time.

INDIAN WRAPS

serves 6

GRILLED TOFU

1 14-OUNCE CAN COCONUT MILK

¾ CUP SHOYU OR TAMARI SOY SAUCE

½ CUP BROWN RICE VINEGAR

¼ CUP CHOPPED CILANTRO

1 JALAPEÑO PEPPER, SEEDED AND CHOPPED

1 TABLESPOON PEELED AND CHOPPED FRESH GINGER

¼ CUP AGAVE NECTAR

2 TEASPOONS CURRY POWDER

½ TEASPOON GROUND CARDAMOM

½ TEASPOON TURMERIC

1 TEASPOON GROUND CORIANDER

½ TEASPOON CAYENNE

1 POUND EXTRA-FIRM TOFU, CUT INTO 6 PIECES

BLACK-EYED PEA SALAD

1 ½ CUPS COOKED BLACK-EYED PEAS (SEE CHART, PAGE 211)

½ CUP FINELY SLICED SCALLIONS

MIXED PEPPER SAUTÉ

2 TABLESPOONS TOASTED SESAME OIL OR PEANUT OIL

4 ASSORTED BELL PEPPERS (GREEN, RED, YELLOW, AND/OR ORANGE), SEEDED, DEVEINED, AND CUT INTO THIN STRIPS

1 RED ONION, PEELED AND THINLY SLICED

SAUTÉED GREENS

3 TABLESPOONS EXTRA-VIRGIN OLIVE OIL

½ CUP CHOPPED ONION

1 TEASPOON TOMATO PASTE

¼ CUP FRESH LEMON JUICE

PINCH OF BLACK PEPPER

2 BUNCHES OF KALE OR MUSTARD GREENS, RINSED, STEMMED, AND COARSELY CHOPPED

6 FLOUR TORTILLAS

1 ½ CUPS COOKED BASMATI RICE (SEE CHART, PAGE 210)

1. Place the coconut milk, shoyu or tamari soy sauce, vinegar, ¾ cup of water, cilantro, jalapeño, ginger, agave nectar, curry powder, cardamom, turmeric, coriander, and cayenne in a blender and blend until smooth.

2. Blanch the tofu in boiling water for 30 seconds, then drain. Place the tofu slices in a single layer in a dish and pour the marinade over to cover. Let stand 1 hour or up to overnight. Remove the tofu with a slotted spoon, reserving the marinade for the black-eyed pea salad.

3. Prepare a charcoal, gas, or stovetop grill. Grill the tofu on each side for about 3 to 5 minutes, or until seared. (You can also broil the tofu on a baking sheet for 3 to 5 minutes per side, until golden brown.) Set aside.

4. Mix the cooked black-eyed peas together with the scallions, then stir in half of the reserved marinade and mix well to combine. Set aside.

5. To make the mixed pepper sauté, in a skillet, heat the sesame oil and sauté the peppers and sliced red onion over medium heat until softened, 6 to 8 minutes. Set aside.

6. To make the sautéed greens, heat the olive oil in a skillet, add the chopped onion, and sauté until tender, about 5 minutes. Stir in the tomato paste and cook for 3 minutes. Add the lemon juice, black pepper to taste, and the greens. Cover and cook, stirring occasionally, until the greens are cooked through, about 6 to 8 minutes. Set aside.

7. To assemble the wraps, place a flour tortilla on a work surface. Put a portion of the tofu a little lower than halfway down the tortilla and top with ¼ cup each of the black-eyed pea salad, the rice, peppers, and greens. Fold the sides in toward the center and roll firmly from bottom to top. Slice on the diagonal and serve.

MEXICAN WRAPS

serves 6

GRILLED TOFU

1 CUP ORANGE JUICE

½ CUP LIME JUICE

¼ CUP AGAVE NECTAR

¼ CUP CHOPPED CILANTRO

1 TEASPOON CUMIN

¼ TEASPOON CHIPOTLE PEPPER POWDER OR CHILI POWDER

1 POUND EXTRA-FIRM TOFU, CUT INTO 6 PIECES

AVOCADO SALAD

3 RIPE AVOCADOS, PEELED, PITTED, AND COARSELY CHOPPED

2 LARGE TOMATOES, COARSELY CHOPPED

1 ONION, FINELY DICED

1 BUNCH OF RED RADISHES, SCRUBBED AND QUARTERED

1 JALAPEÑO PEPPER, SEEDED AND FINELY CHOPPED

¼ CUP FINELY CHOPPED CILANTRO

6 LARGE FLOUR TORTILLAS

1½ CUPS COOKED BLACK BEANS (SEE CHART, PAGE 211)

1½ CUPS COOKED QUINOA (SEE CHART, PAGE 210)

1. Place the orange juice, lime juice, ½ cup of water, agave nectar, cilantro, cumin, and chipotle powder in a blender and blend until well combined.

2. Blanch the tofu in boiling water for 30 seconds, then drain. Place the tofu slices in a single layer in a dish and pour the marinade over to cover. Let stand for 1 hour or up to overnight. Remove the tofu with a slotted spoon, reserving the marinade for the avocado salad.

3. Prepare a charcoal, gas, or stovetop grill. Grill the tofu on each side for about 3 to 5 minutes, or until seared. (You can also broil the tofu for 3 to 5 minutes, or until golden brown.)

4. In a large bowl, mix the avocados, tomatoes, onion, radishes, pepper, and cilantro together until well combined. Stir in about ½ cup of the reserved marinade and mix well to combine.

5. To assemble the wraps, place a flour tortilla on a work surface. Put a portion of the tofu a little lower than halfway down the tortilla, and top with ¼ cup each of avocado salad, black beans, and quinoa. Fold the sides in toward the center and roll firmly from bottom to top. Slice on the diagonal and serve.

MIDDLE EASTERN WRAPS

serves 6

GRILLED TOFU AND EGGPLANT

1 ⅓ CUPS EXTRA-VIRGIN OLIVE OIL

⅓ CUP RED WINE VINEGAR

6 TABLESPOONS CHOPPED FRESH MINT

1 TABLESPOON GROUND CUMIN

½ TEASPOON SEA SALT

¼ TEASPOON PEPPER

1 POUND EXTRA-FIRM TOFU, CUT LENGTHWISE INTO 6 PIECES

1 MEDIUM EGGPLANT, HALVED AND CUT LENGTHWISE INTO 3 PIECES

EXTRA-VIRGIN OLIVE OIL

CHICKPEA SALAD

1 ½ CUPS COOKED CHICKPEAS (SEE CHART, PAGE 211)

½ CUP PITTED AND CHOPPED BLACK OLIVES

½ CUP FINELY CHOPPED RED ONION

1 CUCUMBER, PEELED, SEEDED, AND FINELY CHOPPED

¼ CUP FINELY CHOPPED PARSLEY

2 TABLESPOONS MINCED GARLIC

6 TOMATO-FLAVORED OR WHOLE WHEAT FLOUR TORTILLAS

1 ½ CUPS COOKED COUSCOUS (SEE CHART, PAGE 210)

1. Place the olive oil, vinegar, mint, cumin, salt, and pepper in a blender and blend until well combined.

2. Blanch the tofu for 30 seconds, then drain. Place the tofu slices in a single layer in a dish and pour the marinade over to cover. Let stand for 1 hour or up to overnight. Remove the tofu with a slotted spoon, reserving the marinade for the chickpea salad.

3. Prepare a charcoal, gas, or stovetop grill. Grill the tofu on each side for about 3 to 5 minutes, or until seared. (The tofu can also be broiled on a baking sheet for 3 to 5 minutes per side, or until golden brown.) Set aside. Brush the eggplant slices with olive oil and grill until just tender and lightly browned, about 5 to 7 minutes per side. (The eggplant can also be placed on an oiled baking sheet and broiled for 5 to 7 minutes, or until lightly browned.)

4. Place the cooked chickpeas, olives, onion, cucumber, parsley, and garlic in a bowl and mix well. Stir in half of the reserved marinade and mix well to combine.

5. To assemble the wraps, place a flour tortilla on a work surface. Put a portion of the tofu a little lower than halfway down the tortilla, and top with ¼ cup each of the chickpea salad, the couscous, and a slice of the grilled eggplant. Fold the sides in toward the center and roll firmly from bottom to top. Slice on the diagonal and serve.

MAIN COURSES

When our nonvegetarian guests sample our main courses, they are always amazed at how truly varied and satisfying vegan food can be. Our daily pasta special may be a "live" pasta made entirely of raw ingredients or fresh gnocchi smothered with creamy Tofu Alfredo Sauce. Homemade seitan is served in a variety of ways—with white wine and caper sauce or topped with Wild Mushroom Gravy. Our stir-fries are filled with the flavor of farm-fresh vegetables and Ginger-Miso Sauce or Spicy Soba Noodles. And warming comfort foods, such as Paradise Casserole and Tofu Potpie, are always an essential part of the menu.

This is vegan cooking at its creative best. It proves that main courses served in restaurants and at home need not be based on meat or seafood.

PARADISE CASSEROLE

serves 6 to 8

ise Casserole has been one of the most popular dishes we've served at the
ant over the years. It is a delicious combination of cinnamon-scented sweet
potatoes layered with black beans and millet. This is wonderfully hearty, loaded with
complex carbohydrates, vitamins, and protein. Enjoy!

4   SWEET POTATOES

1   TABLESPOON SWEET WHITE MISO

1   TEASPOON UMEBOSHI VINEGAR

2   TEASPOONS GROUND CINNAMON

1   CUP BLACK BEANS, SOAKED
    OVERNIGHT WITH A 1-INCH PIECE
    OF KOMBU, DRAINED

2   TEASPOONS MINCED GARLIC

½   CUP FINELY CHOPPED WHITE ONION

1   TEASPOON CUMIN
    PINCH OF CRUSHED RED PEPPER
    PINCH OF SEA SALT

1½ CUPS MILLET

1   TABLESPOON EXTRA-VIRGIN OLIVE OIL

1. Preheat the oven to 350°F.

2. Bake the sweet potatoes for 1 hour, or until fork-tender. When cool enough to handle,
   remove the cooked potatoes from their skins, place them in a large mixing bowl, and mash
   with a potato masher until smooth. Combine the miso, vinegar, and cinnamon with the
   potatoes.

3. Meanwhile, put the beans in a large stockpot and add water to cover by 2 inches. Add the
   garlic, onion, cumin, crushed red pepper, and salt and bring to a boil over high heat.
   Reduce the heat, cover, and simmer the beans for 45 to 60 minutes, or until tender. Drain and
   set aside.

4. While the beans are cooking, put the millet and 4 cups of salted water in a large pot and
   bring to a boil. Then cover and simmer over low heat for 45 minutes, or until the water is
   absorbed. Set aside.

5. Lightly oil a large baking pan or casserole. Spread the millet over the bottom of the pan,
   then spread the black beans in an even layer over the millet. Top with the sweet potato
   mixture over the black beans in an even layer.

6. Bake the casserole for 45 minutes. Remove from the oven and let cool a bit before serving.

"LIVE" PASTA WITH RED PEPPER MARINARA

serves 6 to 8

"Live Food" is a form of veganism where fruits, vegetables, nuts, seeds, grains, and beans are not cooked. Some believe that all foods should be served in their natural state and that cooking diminishes the foods' amount of vitamins, minerals, and enzymes. We believe in serving a balance of both cooked and live food. Here is an interesting and delicious recipe of raw vegetables sliced into "noodles" and served as pasta. You'll need a mandoline or a very sharp knife to slice the vegetables very thinly.

4 MEDIUM ZUCCHINI, PEELED

4 MEDIUM YELLOW SQUASH, PEELED

2 RED BELL PEPPERS, HALVED, SEEDED, AND DEVEINED

3 RIPE TOMATOES, QUARTERED

2 SHALLOTS, PEELED

¼ CUP CHOPPED FRESH BASIL LEAVES

1 CUP SUN-DRIED TOMATOES, REHYDRATED (SEE NOTE)

2 TABLESPOONS CHOPPED FRESH OREGANO

1 TABLESPOON FINELY CHOPPED FRESH THYME LEAVES

2 GARLIC CLOVES

¼ CUP PITTED KALAMATA OLIVES

¼ CUP RED WINE

2 TABLESPOONS WHITE MISO

2 TABLESPOONS AGAVE NECTAR (OPTIONAL)

2 TEASPOONS FRESHLY GROUND BLACK PEPPER

½ CUP THINLY SLICED FENNEL, FOR GARNISH

¼ CUP PINE NUTS, FOR GARNISH

KALAMATA OLIVES, FOR GARNISH

1. Using a mandoline or a very sharp knife, slice the zucchini and squash lengthwise into long paper-thin rectangles. Slice the rectangles into ribbons to make pasta "noodles."

2. Combine the peppers, tomatoes, shallots, basil, sun-dried tomatoes, oregano, thyme, garlic, olives, wine, miso, ½ cup of water, agave nectar, and pepper in a food processor and purée until smooth.

3. Spoon the sauce over the pasta and garnish with the fennel, pine nuts, and olives.

NOTE: To rehydrate sun-dried tomatoes, soak in hot water to cover until softened, about 15 to 20 minutes. Drain well.

POTATO GNOCCHI
WITH TOFU ALFREDO SAUCE

serves 6 to 8

Gnocchi, those tasty little Italian potato dumplings, aren't difficult to make as long as you work quickly to roll out the dough. We usually use freshly roasted red peppers in this recipe, but you can also use good-quality roasted peppers from a jar.

---

2 POUNDS IDAHO OR YUKON GOLD
POTATOES, PEELED AND CUT INTO
1-INCH CUBES

½ CUP FINELY CHOPPED ROASTED
RED PEPPERS

½ CUP SUN-DRIED TOMATOES,
REHYDRATED (SEE NOTE, PAGE 111)
AND FINELY CHOPPED

½ CUP FINELY CHOPPED FRESH BASIL

PINCH OF SEA SALT

2 CUPS WHOLE WHEAT PASTRY FLOUR

TOFU ALFREDO SAUCE (RECIPE
FOLLOWS)

1. In a large pot, place the potatoes, cover with cold water, and bring to a boil. Reduce the heat slightly and cook until tender, about 20 to 30 minutes. Drain the potatoes thoroughly and return them to the pan. Add the peppers, sun-dried tomatoes, basil, and salt and mash well until almost lump-free. Add the flour ¼ cup at a time and mix thoroughly. The dough should be smooth and not too dry.

2. Cut the dough into thirds. Flour your hands and the work surface and roll the dough into a rope about ½ inch thick. Cut off 1-inch pieces and put your thumbprint into each piece, making an indentation.

3. Bring a large pot of water to a boil. Add the gnocchi and boil for approximately 2 minutes, until they rise to the surface. Remove with a slotted spoon. Serve at once with warm Tofu Alfredo Sauce or another sauce of your choice.

TOFU ALFREDO SAUCE

makes 2 to 2½ cups

Here's a really easy sauce that's great for vegans who want a delicious, creamy-textured topping for gnocchi or pasta.

1 POUND SILKEN TOFU

1 HEAD OF GARLIC, PEELED

¼ CUP SESAME TAHINI

¼ CUP SHOYU OR TAMARI SOY SAUCE

PINCH OF SALT

Blend all of the ingredients with 1 cup of water in a blender or food processor until smooth. Transfer to a saucepan and cook for an hour over medium-low heat, stirring occasionally. Serve warm over gnocchi or pasta.

VEGETABLE LASAGNA WITH HERBED TOFU RICOTTA

serves 8 to 10

Here is a delicious vegetarian lasagna made with a combination of herbed tofu ricotta, grilled vegetables, and homemade Marinara Sauce. Serve with a salad of mixed greens and crusty bread. Mangia!

HERBED TOFU RICOTTA

- 1 POUND FIRM TOFU, RINSED
- 1 TEASPOON DRIED BASIL
- 1 TEASPOON DRIED THYME
- 1 TEASPOON DRIED OREGANO
- 2 TEASPOONS SEA SALT
- ½ TEASPOON FRESHLY GROUND BLACK PEPPER

GRILLED ZUCCHINI AND EGGPLANT

- 6 TABLESPOONS EXTRA-VIRGIN OLIVE OIL
- 4 TABLESPOONS BALSAMIC VINEGAR
- 1 TEASPOON CHOPPED GARLIC
  PINCH OF SEA SALT
  PINCH OF BLACK PEPPER

- 2 MEDIUM ZUCCHINI, SLICED LENGTH-WISE INTO ¼-INCH-THICK SLICES
- 1 LARGE EGGPLANT, SLICED LENGTHWISE INTO ¼-INCH-THICK SLICES

SAUTÉED MUSHROOMS AND ONIONS

- 3 TABLESPOONS EXTRA-VIRGIN OLIVE OIL
- 1 TEASPOON GARLIC
- 1 CUP FINELY CHOPPED ONIONS
- 1 CUP FINELY CHOPPED MUSHROOMS SEA SALT
- 12 PIECES SEMOLINA OR ARTICHOKE LASAGNA
- 1 CUP MARINARA SAUCE (PAGE 163)
- 1 CUP GRATED SOY CHEESE (OPTIONAL)

1. Combine the tofu, basil, thyme, oregano, salt, and pepper in a food processor and process until smooth. Add a bit of water if the mixture seems too dry. Refrigerate until ready to use.

2. In a mixing bowl, whisk together the olive oil, balsamic vinegar, garlic, salt, and pepper and set aside.

3. Prepare a charcoal, gas, or stovetop grill. Lightly brush the zucchini and eggplant with the olive oil mixture and grill the vegetables for about 4 to 5 minutes per side. Set aside.

4. In a large sauté pan, heat 2 tablespoons of the olive oil. Add the garlic, onions, and mushrooms and cook over medium heat until just softened, about 4 to 5 minutes. Set aside.

5. Preheat the oven to 350°F.

6. In a large soup pot, bring 2 quarts of water to a boil. Add sea salt to taste and the remaining tablespoon of olive oil. Add the lasagna noodles and cook at a rolling boil until just tender, about 8 to 10 minutes. Remove and cool, then rinse the noodles with cold water. Drain and set aside.

7. To assemble the lasagna, spoon a bit of marinara sauce over the bottom of a 9 × 13-inch baking pan and arrange a row of 4 noodles in the pan. Top with a layer of the grilled zucchini and eggplant, then top with a layer of the mushrooms and onions, then spoon a layer of the tofu ricotta over it. Spoon the Marinara Sauce over the ricotta and repeat the layering once more. Top with a layer of noodles and Marinara Sauce. Bake for 45 minutes, or until bubbly.

8. Remove from the oven and immediately sprinkle with grated soy cheese, if using, while the lasagna is still very hot.

MUSHROOM RISOTTO

serves 4

We enjoy cooking risotto for intimate dinners with friends. The secret to perfect, creamy risotto is to use the right kind of rice and stir the broth diligently while the rice is simmering.

½ CUP DRY WHITE WINE

2 CUPS VEGETABLE BROTH (PAGE 38)

2 TABLESPOONS SOY MARGARINE

½ TEASPOON MINCED GARLIC

2 CUPS THINLY SLICED WHITE MUSHROOMS

1 SMALL RED OR YELLOW BELL PEPPER, SEEDED, DEVEINED, AND THINLY SLICED

FRESHLY GROUND BLACK PEPPER

1 CUP ARBORIO RICE

4 TABLESPOONS GRATED SOY MOZZARELLA CHEESE

1. In a saucepan, combine the wine, broth, and 1 cup of water. Bring to a boil, then simmer over very low heat.

2. In a large soup pot over medium heat, melt the soy margarine. Add the garlic, mushrooms, bell pepper, black pepper to taste, and rice and stir until well coated. Add ½ cup of the simmering broth, bring to a boil, reduce the heat, and simmer gently, stirring frequently, until most of the liquid is absorbed. Continue adding the liquid in ½-cup increments and stirring until the rice has absorbed it all. This will take approximately 20 to 25 minutes. The rice is done when it is creamy and not soupy. It will be tender, not mushy, and will retain its bite.

3. Divide the risotto among 4 large soup bowls, sprinkle with the grated mozzarella, and serve at once.

VARIATION: To make risotto cakes, let the cooked risotto cool and firm up. Then shape the risotto into 2-inch-wide patties and sauté in olive oil until golden on both sides.

HOMEMADE SEITAN STE

serves 6

Seitan is readily available in health food markets, but we prefer to make
from scratch. The basic ingredients are simple—just whole wheat and u
white flours and water. Marinating the seitan is a crucial step; it's time-cc
the result is well worth it. We like to serve these steaks with Wild Mushroom Gravy
(page 165). Joy has lots of fun making this with her niece Laura and her nephew Grant.

SEITAN STEAKS

- 4 CUPS WHOLE WHEAT BREAD FLOUR
- 4 CUPS UNBLEACHED WHITE FLOUR
- 6 CUPS ROASTED VEGETABLE BROTH
  (PAGE 39), OR ANY OTHER
  VEGETABLE BROTH

MARINADE

- 2 CUPS EXTRA-VIRGIN OLIVE OIL
- 1 CUP SHOYU OR TAMARI SOY SAUCE
- ½ CUP DIJON MUSTARD
- 16 GARLIC CLOVES, MINCED
- 1 TABLESPOON FRESHLY GROUND
  BLACK PEPPER
- 2 TEASPOONS HOT SAUCE

1. Combine the 2 flours in a large mixing bowl. Mix the flour with enough water to make a stiff dough. Gather into a ball and knead vigorously on a floured surface for at least 13 minutes. Place in a bowl and cover the dough with cold water. Let stand for ½ hour or up to overnight in the refrigerator.

2. Pour off the water and cover again with fresh cold water. Knead the dough under the water to wash out the starch and some of the bran. Pour off the milky white water and cover with fresh water. Keep washing and rinsing while kneading the dough until the water becomes almost clear. Divide the dough in half, place the halves in a large stockpot, and cover with the 6 cups of broth. Bring to a boil, then turn down the heat and simmer for 1½ to 2 hours. Remove from the heat and set aside to cool (see Note). Slice the dough into "steaks" and place in a large baking dish.

3. Place the olive oil, shoyu or tamari soy sauce, mustard, garlic, pepper, and hot sauce in a blender and blend until smooth. Pour over the seitan and marinate in the refrigerator for at least 2 hours.

4. Prepare a charcoal, gas, or stovetop grill. Grill the seitan steaks over medium-high heat until golden brown, about 4 minutes per side.

NOTE: If not using immediately, store the seitan in the broth in the refrigerator. The seitan can also be drained and frozen.

PECAN-CRUSTED SEITAN

serves 4 to 6

This is a very versatile dish that we've made in many ways. In addition to coating the seitan cutlets with pecans, you can also use walnuts, sesame seeds, or pumpkin seeds. Serve with Marinara Sauce (page 163), Garlic Mashed Potatoes (page 145), and Sautéed Mixed Greens (page 147). Very tasty!

MARINADE

¾ CUP TOMATO PASTE

¼ CUP UMEBOSHI VINEGAR

¼ CUP RED WINE

½ CUP ORANGE JUICE

¼ CUP SHOYU OR TAMARI SOY SAUCE

¼ CUP MINCED GARLIC

¼ CUP CHOPPED PARSLEY

2 TABLESPOONS MINCED FRESH TARRAGON

2 TABLESPOONS MINCED FRESH ROSEMARY

8 TO 10 SEITAN CUTLETS (ABOUT 1 POUND), PREFERABLY HOMEMADE (SEE PAGE 117)

2 CUPS ALL-PURPOSE FLOUR

½ TEASPOON SEA SALT

½ TEASPOON FRESHLY GROUND BLACK PEPPER

1 CUP GROUND PECANS

2 TABLESPOONS FINELY CHOPPED FRESH ROSEMARY

¼ CUP EXTRA-VIRGIN OLIVE OIL

1. Place the tomato paste, vinegar, wine, orange juice, shoyu or tamari soy sauce, garlic, parsley, tarragon, and minced rosemary in a blender and blend until smooth. Pour the marinade over the seitan and marinate in the refrigerator at least 3 hours or up to overnight.

2. In a shallow bowl, mix together the flour, salt, pepper, pecans, and chopped rosemary. Dredge the cutlets.

3. Heat the oil in a sauté pan and sauté the cutlets until golden brown, about 2 to 3 minutes per side. Serve at once with the desired sauce.

SEITAN PICCATA WITH WHITE WINE AND CAPER S

serves 4 to 6

This is an easy and elegant entrée with a sauce flavored with white
shallots, and parsley, among other good things. We like to serve it w...
and roasted vegetables.

6 SEITAN CUTLETS (ABOUT 4 OUNCES
  EACH), PREFERABLY HOMEMADE
  (PAGE 117)
  WHOLE WHEAT FLOUR, FOR
  DREDGING
¼ CUP EXTRA-VIRGIN OLIVE OIL
½ CUP DICED SHALLOTS
½ CUP DICED ONIONS
1 TEASPOON CHOPPED GARLIC
¼ CUP DRAINED CAPERS

1 CUP DRY WHITE WINE
¼ CUP FRESH LEMON JUICE
1 CUP VEGETABLE BROTH, PREFERABLY
  HOMEMADE (SEE PAGE 38)
2 TABLESPOONS UNBLEACHED FLOUR
4 TABLESPOONS SOY MARGARINE
1 CUP CHOPPED PARSLEY
1 TEASPOON SEA SALT
½ TEASPOON FRESHLY GROUND BLACK
  PEPPER

1. Dredge the seitan cutlets in the flour, shaking off any excess. In a sauté pan, heat 2 tablespoons of the olive oil over high heat and sauté the cutlets until crisp and golden brown,
   about 30 seconds per side. Place each cutlet on individual plates or a platter.

2. Heat the remaining olive oil in the pan. Add the shallots, onions, garlic, and capers, sauté,
   and stir until softened, about 1 to 2 minutes. Add the wine and cook until reduced by half.
   Whisk in the lemon juice and allow to reduce a bit more.

3. Add the broth and the unbleached flour and bring to a boil. Reduce the heat and simmer
   for about 1 minute. Whisk in the margarine, parsley, salt, and pepper. Pour over the seitan
   cutlets and serve at once.

TEMPEH SCALLOPINI WITH SHALLOTS AND MUSHROOMS

serves 6

Our lemony, aromatic scallopini is made with soy rice tempeh, which is made from wild rice and is available at health food markets. Of course, you can make this using any kind of tempeh and it will still taste delicious. We like to serve it with roasted red potatoes and steamed asparagus.

MARINADE

- ¼ CUP SHOYU OR TAMARI SOY SAUCE
- 2½ CUPS WATER
- 1 GARLIC CLOVE, MINCED
- 1 1-INCH PIECE OF KOMBU (OPTIONAL)
- 2 BAY LEAVES

- 2 8-OUNCE PACKAGES SOY RICE TEMPEH OR ANOTHER TYPE OF TEMPEH
- ¼ CUP EXTRA-VIRGIN OLIVE OIL
- 2 GARLIC CLOVES, THINLY SLICED
- 4 SHALLOTS, THINLY SLICED
- ½ POUND WHITE BUTTON MUSHROOMS, THINLY SLICED
- 1 CUP UNBLEACHED ALL-PURPOSE FLOUR
- JUICE OF 2 LEMONS
- ½ CUP RED WINE

1. Preheat the oven to 375°F.

2. In a mixing bowl, combine the shoyu or tamari soy sauce, water, garlic, kombu (if using), and bay leaves and stir well. Cut the tempeh in half lengthwise, then cut into thirds to make 6 pieces per package. Place the tempeh in a baking dish and pour the marinade over it. Cover with foil and bake for 30 minutes. Remove from the oven and set aside to cool, reserving the liquid.

3. In a large sauté pan, heat the olive oil and add the garlic, shallots, and mushrooms. Cook over medium heat until tender, about 5 minutes. Remove the mushroom mixture with a slotted spoon and set aside.

4. Put the flour in a large shallow bowl or on a plate and dredge the tempeh pieces. Add the reserved marinade to the pan and heat through. Add the tempeh pieces to the sauté pan and cook over medium heat until the tempeh is nicely browned, about 3 to 4 minutes per side. Remove and keep warm.

5. Add the lemon juice and red wine to the sauté pan and simmer until the liquid is reduced by half. Stir in the mushroom mixture and heat through.

6. Spoon the sauce over the reserved tempeh and serve at once.

CORNMEAL-CRUSTED TEMPEH

serves 4

Earthy tempeh is a mainstay of many of our main courses. This dish pairs very nicely
with Sweet Potato Smash (page 144) and sautéed kale, and it is wonderful
when served with a side of Candle Café Barbecued Beans (page 152).

- 2 8-OUNCE PACKAGES TEMPEH, EACH CUT INTO THIRDS
- ½ CUP SHOYU OR TAMARI SOY SAUCE
- 3 TABLESPOONS MAPLE SYRUP
- 1 TABLESPOON MINCED GARLIC
- 3 SLICES OF FRESH GINGER
- ½ CUP MEDIUM- TO FINE-GROUND CORNMEAL
- 1 TEASPOON CRUSHED RED PEPPER FLAKES
- 1 TEASPOON DRIED THYME
- 1 TEASPOON DRIED OREGANO
- 1 TEASPOON GROUND CUMIN
- PINCH OF SEA SALT
- ½ CUP EXTRA-VIRGIN OLIVE OIL

1. Preheat the oven to 350°F.

2. Place the tempeh in a baking dish. In a small bowl, whisk together the shoyu or tamari soy sauce, ½ cup of water, the maple syrup, garlic, and ginger and pour over the tempeh. Cover and bake for 1 hour. Remove from the oven and set aside to cool. Drain and cut the tempeh into halves or triangles.

3. In a large shallow bowl, mix together the cornmeal, red pepper flakes, thyme, oregano, cumin, and sea salt. Dip the tempeh pieces into the cornmeal mixture to coat.

4. In a large skillet, heat the oil over medium-high heat until very hot. Cook the coated tempeh until golden brown, about a minute per side.

5. Remove from the heat and serve at once.

CURRIED COCONUT BEGGARS' PURSES

serves 6 to 8

Chef Mark Felix from the Plaza Hotel created this dish as an appetizer. We like it so much that we've adapted the recipe and serve it as an entrée at our restaurant.

- 2 TABLESPOONS SESAME OIL
- 4 GARLIC CLOVES, FINELY MINCED
- 2 TABLESPOONS FINELY CHOPPED FRESH GINGER
- 4 SCALLIONS, FINELY CHOPPED
- ½ CUP FINELY DICED CARROTS
- ½ CUP FINELY DICED GREEN BELL PEPPER
- ½ CUP FINELY DICED RED BELL PEPPER
- 1 BAY LEAF
- 1 POUND SEITAN, CUT INTO SMALL STRIPS

- 1 CUP WHITE WINE
- 1 14-OUNCE CAN COCONUT MILK
- ½ CUP CHOPPED CILANTRO
- 4 FRESH BASIL LEAVES, FINELY CHOPPED
- 1 TEASPOON SEA SALT
  PINCH OF CAYENNE
- 1 TEASPOON CURRY POWDER
- ¼ CUP FINELY CHOPPED FRESH CHIVES
- 8 SHEETS OF PHYLLO DOUGH, THAWED IF FROZEN
  EXTRA-VIRGIN OLIVE OIL, FOR BRUSHING

1. Preheat the oven to 350°F.

2. In a large sauté pan over medium heat, heat the sesame oil. Cook the garlic, ginger, scallions, carrots, peppers, and bay leaf over medium heat for 5 minutes. Add the seitan strips, white wine, and coconut milk to the mixture and cook for 5 to 6 more minutes. Add the cilantro, basil, salt, cayenne, curry powder, and chives and continue cooking, stirring occasionally, for 20 minutes. Remove the bay leaf and set aside to cool.

3. Take 1 sheet of phyllo dough and fold it in half lengthwise. Brush with a bit of olive oil. Place ½ cup of the filling into the center of the phyllo sheet. Twist the dough so that it gathers to make a bundle, or "purse." Repeat with the remaining dough, oil, and filling to make 6 to 8 purses.

4. Place the purses on a baking sheet and bake for 20 minutes, until golden brown. Serve at once.

GINGER-MISO STIR-FRY

serves 4 to 6

Stir-fries are so versatile and fun to make. We like to use the freshest
vegetables we can find from local farmer's and Asian markets. Feel free to
improvise your own stir-fry, using your favorite vegetables in this quick
and easy recipe. Serve over brown rice or soba noodles.

GINGER-MISO SAUCE

- 1 TABLESPOON MINCED GARLIC
- ¼ CUP MINCED FRESH GINGER
- ½ CUP MELLOW WHITE MISO
- ¼ CUP AGAVE NECTAR
- ¼ CUP SHOYU OR TAMARI SOY SAUCE
- 2 TABLESPOONS TOASTED SESAME OIL
  PINCH OF CRUSHED RED PEPPER
  FLAKES

STIR-FRY

- 3 TABLESPOONS EXTRA-VIRGIN OLIVE OIL OR WATER
- 1½ TEASPOONS MINCED GARLIC
- 1½ TEASPOONS MINCED FRESH GINGER
- ½ CUP SEEDED, DEVEINED, AND SLICED RED BELL PEPPER
- ½ CUP SEEDED AND SLICED YELLOW BELL PEPPER
- ¾ CUP SLICED ONION
- ½ CUP SLICED BLANCHED BOK CHOY
- ½ CUP BLANCHED STRING BEANS, CHOPPED
- 1½ CUPS BLANCHED BROCCOLI, CHOPPED
- 1 CUP CHOPPED SHREDDED CABBAGE
- ½ CUP STEMMED AND SLICED SHIITAKE MUSHROOMS
- 1 CUP RINSED, DRAINED, AND CUBED EXTRA-FIRM TOFU
- ¼ CUP THINLY SLICED WATER CHESTNUTS
- ¼ CUP SESAME SEEDS

1. To make the ginger-miso sauce, place all of the ingredients with 1 cup of water in a blender and blend until smooth. The sauce will keep in the refrigerator, covered, for up to a week.

2. In a large sauté pan or wok, heat the olive oil over high heat. Add the garlic and ginger and sauté for about 2 minutes.

3. Add the vegetables and tofu and toss to combine. Continue to sauté and toss the vegetables and tofu together until they reach the desired doneness, about 5 to 10 minutes, depending on your taste.

4. Add the ginger-miso sauce and water chestnuts and stir-fry for an additional 3 minutes. Sprinkle with sesame seeds and serve at once.

SPICY SOBA NOODLE STIR-FRY

serves 6 to 8

We like to experiment with stir-fries and this is one of our favorite creations.
Although the ingredient list is long, it's easy to make, especially since
the peanut sauce can be made well ahead of time.

PEANUT SAUCE

1 ½ CUPS SMOOTH PEANUT BUTTER

¼ CUP BROWN RICE VINEGAR

1 SMALL RED ONION, FINELY CHOPPED

2 TABLESPOONS FINELY CHOPPED
CILANTRO

2 TABLESPOONS FINELY CHOPPED
FRESH GINGER

1 GARLIC CLOVE, MINCED

1 TABLESPOON CRUSHED RED CHILI
FLAKES

1 TABLESPOON KETCHUP

¼ CUP SHOYU OR TAMARI SOY SAUCE

1 TABLESPOON HOT SAUCE

¼ CUP AGAVE NECTAR

1 TABLESPOON SESAME OIL

SOBA NOODLES AND TEMPEH

1 8-OUNCE PACKAGE TEMPEH, CUBED

PINCH OF SEA SALT

1 TEASPOON EXTRA-VIRGIN OLIVE OIL

1 POUND SOBA NOODLES OR THIN
PASTA

STIR-FRY

3 TABLESPOONS EXTRA-VIRGIN
OLIVE OIL

2 TEASPOONS MINCED GARLIC

2 TEASPOONS MINCED FRESH GINGER

¾ CUP CHOPPED ONION

1 CUP SHREDDED GREEN CABBAGE

½ CUP TRIMMED AND BLANCHED
STRING BEANS

1 ½ CUPS CUT AND BLANCHED BROCCOLI
FLORETS

1 RED BELL PEPPER, SEEDED AND
THINLY SLICED

1 GREEN BELL PEPPER, SEEDED AND
THINLY SLICED

½ CUP SLICED BLANCHED BOK CHOY

¼ CUP SLICED SHIITAKE MUSHROOMS

1 TABLESPOON SHOYU OR TAMARI
SOY SAUCE

2 ½ TEASPOONS TOASTED SESAME OIL

1. To prepare the peanut sauce, place all of the ingredients with 2 cups of water in a blender
   and blend until smooth. The sauce will keep in the refrigerator, covered, for up to a week.
   Bring to room temperature before serving.

2. Place the tempeh cubes in a nonreactive bowl and cover with the peanut sauce. Refrigerate
   for at least a half hour or up to overnight. Drain and set aside.

3. To prepare the soba noodles, bring a large soup pot of water to a boil and add the salt
   and olive oil. Add the soba noodles and cook until just tender, about 10 minutes. Drain and
   set aside.

4. To prepare the stir-fry, heat the olive oil in a large sauté pan or wok over high heat. Add tempeh and sauté for 3 to 5 minutes. Add the garlic, ginger, onion, cabbage, string beans, and broccoli and stir-fry for 5 minutes, then add the peppers, bok choy, and mushrooms and sauté for about 2 minutes. Add the peanut sauce and continue to sauté, tossing the vegetables, tempeh cubes, and sauce together until the desired doneness is reached, about 5 to 10 minutes, depending on your taste.

5. Add the shoyu or tamari soy sauce and sesame oil and stir-fry for an additional 3 minutes. Serve the vegetables over the soba noodles with additional peanut sauce, if desired.

NOTE ON STIR-FRYING

Stir-frying is one of the quickest preparation methods and takes only a few minutes if you prepare the ingredients ahead of time. Traditional stir-frying is done in a wok set over a high flame and requires very little fat because the high heat and constant stirring of the food sears in the moisture, flavor, and nutrients.

SOME STIR-FRYING TIPS

- Cut up all ingredients to the same size for even cooking.
- Add the ingredients according to the length of time they need to cook; quick-cooking ingredients go in last.
- Consider color and texture in choosing ingredients for a stir-fry.
- For low-fat stir-frying, substitute water for oil.

TEX-MEX TOSTADAS

serves 6

Our tostadas are made with pinto beans, seitan, and Tofu-Cilantro Sour Cream
layered onto crunchy baked tortillas. It's best to prepare the seitan and
tortillas while the beans are simmering, then assemble the tostadas when
everything is cooked and ready to eat.

---

1 CUP PINTO BEANS, RINSED, DRAINED,
AND SOAKED OVERNIGHT

1 2-INCH PIECE OF DRIED KOMBU

12 6-INCH CORN TORTILLAS

¼ CUP EXTRA-VIRGIN OLIVE OIL

1½ POUNDS SEITAN, SLICED INTO
1-INCH-THICK PIECES

1 TABLESPOON MINCED GARLIC

½ CUP DICED ONION

1 TEASPOON FRESH OR DRIED
OREGANO

1 TEASPOON FRESH OR DRIED THYME
PINCH OF SEA SALT

1½ CUPS SHREDDED ROMAINE LETTUCE

1½ CUPS PICO DE GALLO (PAGE 34)

1 CUP TOFU-CILANTRO SOUR CREAM
(PAGE 167)

1. In a large soup pot, place the beans and kombu and add 8 cups of water. Bring to a boil,
reduce the heat, and simmer until the beans are tender, about 30 minutes. Drain the beans
and remove the kombu.

2. Meanwhile, preheat the oven to 300°F. Place the tortillas on baking sheets and brush with
1 tablespoon olive oil. Bake until crisp, about 20 minutes. Set aside until ready to assemble.

3. Prepare a charcoal, gas, or stovetop grill. Cook the seitan on the grill until nicely browned,
about 3 minutes per side. Shred the grilled seitan in a food processor and set aside.

4. In a sauté pan, heat another tablespoon of olive oil and add the garlic, onion, oregano,
thyme, and salt and sauté for 3 minutes. Add the shredded seitan and sauté for an additional
3 minutes.

5. When the beans are cooked and drained, sauté them with the remaining 2 tablespoons of
oil in a large sauté pan over medium heat for 5 minutes. Transfer the beans to a mixing bowl
and mash them with a fork.

6. To assemble the tostadas, place 2 corn tortillas each on 6 plates. Spread 2 tablespoons
of the refried bean mixture onto each tortilla, then top with 2 tablespoons of the seitan
mixture. Add a small handful of lettuce. Top each tostada plate with the Pico de Gallo and
a dab of Tofu-Cilantro Sour Cream.

PORCINI MUSHROOM STROGANOFF

serves 6

Rich and delicious stroganoff, made with earthy fresh mushrooms, dried porcini
mushrooms, and fettuccine, is a big hit with all of our customers.
Serve this simple yet elegant dish for a warm dinner at home on a cold night.

- 2 TABLESPOONS EXTRA-VIRGIN OLIVE OIL
- 1 TABLESPOON UNBLEACHED FLOUR
- 2 TABLESPOONS SOY MARGARINE
- 3 GARLIC CLOVES, CHOPPED
- 1 YELLOW ONION, FINELY CHOPPED
- 1 TABLESPOON SEA SALT
- 1 TABLESPOON FRESHLY GROUND BLACK PEPPER
- 2 OUNCES DRIED PORCINI MUSHROOMS
- 1 POUND BUTTON MUSHROOMS

- ¼ CUP WHITE WINE
- 1 TABLESPOON TOMATO PASTE
- 1 CUP SOY MILK
- PINCH OF DRIED PARSLEY
- PINCH OF DRIED DILL
- 1 THYME SPRIG
- 1 BAY LEAF
- ½ CUP CHOPPED FRESH CHIVES
- 1 POUND FETTUCCINE

1. In a large saucepan over medium heat, heat the oil. Stir in the flour and cook for 4 minutes, stirring frequently. Add the soy margarine, garlic, onion, salt, and pepper and cook for an additional 4 minutes.

2. Add the porcini and button mushrooms, wine, tomato paste, and soy milk. Stir in the parsley, dill, thyme, bay leaf, and chives. Bring to a boil, then simmer over low heat for 20 minutes.

3. Bring a large pot of water to a boil and cook the fettuccine according to package directions. Drain.

4. Spoon the sauce over the fettuccine and serve at once.

ORY VEGETABLE POTPIE

serves 6 to 8

s is vegan comfort food at its best. Our warm and nourishing potpie,
ith vegetables, herbs, and tofu, is just the right thing for a special dinner
a cold winter's night. You'll need a 1-quart baking dish in which to
bake and serve the potpie.

POTPIE FILLING

- 1 TABLESPOON EXTRA-VIRGIN OLIVE OIL
- 2 GARLIC CLOVES, MINCED
- ½ SWEET POTATO, PEELED AND FINELY DICED
- ½ RUSSET POTATO, PEELED AND FINELY DICED
- 1 SMALL CELERY STALK, FINELY DICED
- ¼ CUP PEELED AND FINELY DICED CARROTS
- ½ CUP FRESH OR FROZEN PEAS
- ¼ CUP PEELED AND FINELY DICED ZUCCHINI
- 1 POUND FIRM TOFU, CUT INTO SMALL CUBES
- ½ CUP WHITE WINE
- 1 CUP SOY MILK
- 2 TABLESPOONS SOY MARGARINE
- 2 TABLESPOONS UNBLEACHED WHITE FLOUR
- 1 TABLESPOON CHOPPED FRESH OR DRIED TARRAGON
- 1 TABLESPOON CHOPPED FRESH OR DRIED CHERVIL (OPTIONAL)
- 1 TABLESPOON CHOPPED PARSLEY
- 1 BAY LEAF
- 1 ROSEMARY SPRIG
- 1 THYME SPRIG
- 1 TABLESPOON SEA SALT
- 1 TABLESPOON FRESHLY GROUND BLACK PEPPER

HERBED CRUST

- 1 CUP WHOLE WHEAT PASTRY FLOUR
- 1 CUP UNBLEACHED FLOUR
- ⅓ CUP SUNFLOWER OIL
- 1 TEASPOON FINELY CHOPPED FRESH BASIL
- 1 TEASPOON FINELY CHOPPED FRESH ROSEMARY
- 1 TEASPOON FINELY CHOPPED FRESH THYME
- PINCH OF SEA SALT
- ⅔ CUP WATER

1. Preheat the oven to 325°F. Grease a 1-quart baking dish.

2. To prepare the potpie filling, heat the olive oil in a large sauté pan. Add the garlic, potatoes, celery, carrots, peas, and zucchini and cook over medium heat for 5 minutes. Add the tofu, wine, soy milk, soy margarine, flour, tarragon, chervil, if using, parsley, bay leaf, rosemary, thyme, salt, and pepper and cook slowly over medium-low heat until the vegetables are tender, about 20 minutes. Remove the bay leaf and set aside.

3. To prepare the crust, mix the whole wheat pastry flour and unbleached flour together in a bowl. Add the oil, herbs, and salt and mix well to form a dough. Add up to ½ cup water if the dough seems too dry.

4. Cut the dough in half and roll into a 13-inch circle. Fit the dough into the baking dish and trim the edges, leaving a ½-inch overhang. Spoon the filling into the bottom crust. Roll out the second half of the dough into a 12-inch circle. Place over the filling and trim the edges of the dough. Make 4 incisions in the top crust with a knife to serve as vents.

5. Bake the potpie for 30 minutes, or until the top of the crust is golden brown. Let stand for 5 minutes before serving.

INDIAN SAMPLER PLATE

serves 6 to 8

The Candle serves an Indian Sampler or Thali Plate every day. This popular platter
consists of a bean masala and a seasonal vegetable curry plus basmati rice pilaf,
cooling cucumber raita, and Date-Raisin Chutney. We also serve chapati bread as an
accompaniment to all of these delectable dishes. If you can't find chapati, pita or
lavash bread are good substitutes. Feel free to make any of these recipes
separately, or make them all together for an Indian feast for a crowd.

CHANA MASALA
INDIAN CHICKPEA STEW

makes about 5 cups

1 TEASPOON BROWN MUSTARD SEEDS

1 TEASPOON CUMIN SEEDS

1 TABLESPOON COCONUT BUTTER OR
VEGETABLE OIL

2 CUPS DICED ONION

2 TABLESPOONS MINCED GARLIC

2 TABLESPOONS MINCED FRESH
GINGER

1 CUP WATER OR VEGETABLE BROTH
(PAGE 38)

1 CUP DICED FRESH TOMATOES

4 CUPS COOKED CHICKPEAS
(SEE PAGE 211)

½ TEASPOON GROUND CLOVES

½ TEASPOON CINNAMON

½ TEASPOON GROUND CARDAMOM

1. Heat a large skillet over high heat. Add the mustard and cumin seeds and cook, stirring
often, until they begin to pop. Add the coconut butter or oil and stir over medium heat for
about a minute. Add the onion, garlic, and ginger and cook for 4 to 5 minutes, until softened. Stir in the water or broth, tomatoes, chickpeas, cloves, cinnamon, and cardamom.

2. Reduce the heat and cook, stirring occasionally, for 45 minutes. Serve at once, or reheat
gently before serving.

EGGPLANT CURRY

makes 3 to 4 cups

¼ CUP EXTRA-VIRGIN OLIVE OIL

2 MEDIUM ONIONS, PEELED AND DICED

4 GARLIC CLOVES, MINCED

1 1-INCH PIECE OF FRESH GINGER, PEELED AND MINCED

1 JALAPEÑO PEPPER, MINCED

2 MEDIUM TOMATOES, SEEDED AND CHOPPED INTO 3/4-INCH PIECES

½ CUP WATER OR VEGETABLE BROTH (PAGE 38)

1 LARGE EGGPLANT, PEELED AND DICED INTO 1-INCH CUBES

1 MEDIUM GREEN OR YELLOW BELL PEPPER, SEEDED AND DICED INTO ¾-INCH CUBES

1 MEDIUM RED BELL PEPPER, SEEDED AND DICED INTO ¾-INCH CUBES

1 TEASPOON SEA SALT

1 TEASPOON TURMERIC

1 TEASPOON GROUND CORIANDER

1 TEASPOON GROUND FENUGREEK

½ TEASPOON GROUND CUMIN

In a sauté pan, heat the oil over medium heat. Add the onions, garlic, ginger, and jalapeño and cook for 5 minutes. Add the tomatoes and cook for 3 minutes. Add the water or broth, eggplant, peppers, salt, turmeric, coriander, fenugreek, and cumin and cook over medium heat, stirring occasionally, for an hour. Taste, adjust the seasonings, and set aside.

YELLOW BASMATI RICE PILAF

makes 5 cups

2 CUPS BASMATI RICE

1 1/2 TEASPOONS BROWN MUSTARD SEEDS

1 1/2 TEASPOONS WHOLE CUMIN SEEDS

2 TABLESPOONS SAFFLOWER OIL

3/4 CUP DICED ONION

1 TABLESPOON MINCED GARLIC

1 CINNAMON STICK

1/2 TEASPOON WHOLE CLOVES

1 TABLESPOON CHOPPED FRESH GINGER

2 TEASPOONS SEA SALT

1 TEASPOON TURMERIC

3 1/2 CUPS WATER

1 CUP BLANCHED CAULIFLOWER FLORETS

1/2 CUP SHREDDED CARROTS

1/2 CUP GOLDEN RAISINS OR CURRANTS

1/2 CUP TOASTED AND CHOPPED WHOLE OR SLIVERED ALMONDS (SEE NOTE)

2 TABLESPOONS MIRIN (JAPANESE RICE WINE)

1. Rinse and drain the rice.

2. Heat a large sauté pan and add the mustard and cumin seeds. Cook, stirring often, until they begin to pop. Add the oil, onion, garlic, cinnamon stick, cloves, and ginger and sauté over medium heat for about 4 minutes.

3. Add the rice, salt, and turmeric and cook, stirring, until the rice is completely coated, about 1 minute. Add the water, stir, cover, and simmer over medium-low heat about 45 minutes.

4. When the rice is tender add the cauliflower, carrots, raisins, almonds, and mirin and stir well. Taste, adjust the seasonings, and keep warm until serving.

NOTE: To toast the almonds, spread them on a baking sheet and toast them in a preheated 350°F oven or toaster oven for about 5 minutes, or until golden brown. Shake the pan once or twice for even toasting. Slide the nuts off the baking sheet to stop the cooking. When cool enough to handle, coarsely chop the almonds.

TOFU CUCUMBER RAITA

makes 2 cups

This is a wonderfully cooling accompaniment to the spicy dishes
that make up the Thali Plate.

---

1 TEASPOON COCONUT BUTTER OR
VEGETABLE OIL

1 SMALL ONION, FINELY CHOPPED

1 TEASPOON GROUND CUMIN

½ TEASPOON SEA SALT

2 LARGE CUCUMBERS, PEELED,
SEEDED, AND SHREDDED

2 POUNDS SILKEN TOFU

¼ CUP SOY MILK

2 TEASPOONS AGAVE NECTAR

1 TEASPOON ARROWROOT POWDER

¼ CUP CHOPPED FRESH MINT,
PREFERABLY SPEARMINT

1. In a sauté pan over medium-low heat, heat the oil. Add the onion, cumin, and salt and cook
for 10 minutes. Stir in the cucumbers and remove from the heat.

2. Place the tofu, soy milk, agave nectar, and arrowroot powder in a blender and blend until
smooth. Stir into the warm cucumber mixture, add the mint, and chill in the refrigerator at
least an hour before serving.

VARIATION: Substitute a 16-ounce container of plain soy yogurt for the tofu and soy
milk. Instead of cooking the other ingredients, just mix them into the yogurt.

DATE-RAISIN CHUTNEY

makes 1 cup

This chutney is a wonderful condiment for our Thali Plate. It can be made
well ahead of serving time—keep it in the refrigerator and use it to
perk up rice, grains, and bread.

½ CUP APPLE CIDER VINEGAR

¼ CUP UNREFINED SUGAR OR AGAVE
   NECTAR

1 CUP PITTED DATES

1 CUP RAISINS

1 ½-INCH PIECE OF FRESH GINGER,
   PEELED AND MINCED

½ TEASPOON GROUND CUMIN

Place all of the ingredients with 1½ cups of water in a saucepan. Bring to a boil, reduce the
heat, and simmer, covered, stirring frequently, until the mixture is reduced and thickened,
about 1 hour. Serve hot or cold. The chutney will keep, covered, in the refrigerator for up
to 2 weeks.

STUFFED WINTER SQUASH

serves 4

Winter squash, stuffed with savory wild rice and mushrooms, is a delightful dish.
Our friend and colleague Benay Vynerib developed this dish when she was
looking to bring a wheat-free dish to a traditional Thanksgiving dinner.
She particularly likes to make it with delicata squash (which has an edible skin),
but it is also very good with butternut or acorn squash. Served with steamed
broccoli or sautéed greens, it makes a healthy, festive entrée.

4 WINTER SQUASH, SUCH AS DELICATA, BUTTERNUT, OR ACORN

SAFFLOWER OR EXTRA-VIRGIN OLIVE OIL, FOR BRUSHING

3 TABLESPOONS MAPLE SYRUP

1 TEASPOON GROUND CINNAMON

WILD RICE STUFFING

2 QUARTS VEGETABLE BROTH (PAGE 38)

3 CUPS WILD RICE, RINSED

PINCH OF SEA SALT

1 TABLESPOON EXTRA-VIRGIN OLIVE OIL

6 LARGE SHALLOTS, CHOPPED

6 GARLIC CLOVES, MINCED

1 POUND WHITE MUSHROOMS, THINLY SLICED

1 TABLESPOON SHOYU OR TAMARI SOY SAUCE OR WHEAT-FREE TAMARI

1 TEASPOON DRIED THYME

FRESHLY GROUND BLACK PEPPER

1 CUP CHOPPED PARSLEY

⅓ CUP CHOPPED FRESH SAGE

WILD MUSHROOM GRAVY (PAGE 165), FOR SERVING

1. Preheat the oven to 350°F.

2. Cut the squash in half and scoop out the seeds. Brush with oil and maple syrup and sprinkle with cinnamon. Bake about 20 minutes, or until just tender.

3. Meanwhile, prepare the stuffing. In a stockpot, bring the broth to a boil. Add the rice and salt to the broth and bring to a boil. Reduce the heat, cover, and simmer for 35 to 45 minutes, or until the water is absorbed. Remove from the heat.

4. In a sauté pan, heat the olive oil, add the shallots and garlic, and cook for about 10 minutes, or until golden. Add the mushrooms and continue to cook, stirring occasionally, until the mushrooms release their juices. Add the shoyu or tamari soy sauce or wheat-free tamari, thyme, and pepper to taste. Continue to cook until the liquid evaporates. Transfer to a bowl with the rice. Add the parsley and sage and toss to combine. Taste and adjust the seasonings, adding more pepper, if necessary.

5. Spoon the stuffing into the baked squash halves and return to the oven. Bake for 15 minutes. Remove and serve at once with Wild Mushroom Gravy.

VEGETABLES AND SIDE DISHES

No meal is complete without a side dish or two of garden-fresh vegetables and a hearty helping of grains or beans. We also like to devise whole meals around a few of these vegetable, grain, and bean dishes, since they're easy and quick to prepare.

Some of our favorite vegetable dishes include Sweet and Simple Sea Vegetable, Roasted Roots, and our house specialty, Garlic Mashed Potatoes. Minty Barley Pilaf is one of our favorite grain recipes. Marinated Grilled Tofu is a great staple to have on hand since it is an important component of a number of our dishes throughout the book.

This chapter has plenty of delicious, healthy vegetable-, grain-, and bean-based dishes for you and your family and friends to savor.

CHINESE CABBAGE SAUTÉ

serves 4 to 6 as a side dish

We enjoy this crunchy cabbage sauté in numerous ways. Sometimes we substitute this for Tofu Cucumber Raita on our Indian Plate in cold-weather months. On St. Patrick's Day, we serve it with Guinness Stout–Marinated Seitan Irish Stew.

1½ TEASPOONS MUSTARD SEEDS

1 TEASPOON CUMIN SEEDS

1 TEASPOON FENNEL SEEDS

½ HEAD OF CHINESE CABBAGE, RINSED AND SLICED INTO 1-INCH PIECES

½ MEDIUM GREEN CABBAGE, RINSED AND SLICED INTO 1-INCH PIECES

2 JALAPEÑO PEPPERS, SEEDED AND DICED

¼ CUP SAFFLOWER OR COCONUT OIL

½ TEASPOON TURMERIC

PINCH OF SEA SALT

1. Heat a skillet over medium-high heat and add the mustard seeds, shaking the pan. Add the cumin and fennel seeds and cook until the seeds begin to pop, about 6 minutes. Set aside to cool.

2. Blanch the cabbage in boiling water for about a minute, then drain. Heat a large sauté pan over medium-high heat and add the jalapeños. Cook for 1 minute, then add the cabbage and cook, stirring often. Add the toasted mustard, cumin, and fennel seeds, oil, turmeric, and salt and sauté for about 5 minutes (the cabbage should retain its crunch). Taste, adjust the seasonings, and serve at once.

LEMON-CARAWAY SLAW

serves 8 to 10 as a side dish

We love this fresh, summery slaw and serve it often. It's a good salad to improvise on—for example, you can add shredded beets, jicama, or fennel to the cabbage. For Asian-style slaw, substitute Asian sesame oil for the flax seed oil, use sesame seeds instead of caraway, and add a bit of arame seaweed.

¼ HEAD OF RED CABBAGE, SHREDDED

¼ HEAD OF GREEN CABBAGE, SHREDDED

1 CUP PEELED AND SHREDDED CARROTS

½ CUP LEMON JUICE

¼ CUP FLAX SEED OIL OR SAFFLOWER OIL

2 TABLESPOONS CARAWAY SEEDS

1 TEASPOON AGAVE NECTAR

PINCH OF SEA SALT

FRESHLY GROUND BLACK PEPPER

1. In a large bowl, toss the shredded cabbages and carrots together.

2. Place the lemon juice, oil, caraway seeds, ¼ cup of water, and the agave nectar in a blender and blend until smooth. Strain, add the liquid to the cabbage mixture, and toss together. Add the salt and pepper to taste and toss again. Taste and adjust the seasonings. If not serving immediately, chill in the refrigerator. The slaw is best served the day it's made.

COCONUTTY BABY BOK CHOY

serves 4 to 6 as a side dish

This is a delicious and simple way to serve bok choy. The sauce, which is also great to serve with any sautéed or blanched greens, can be made well ahead of time and then drizzled over the quick-cooked bok choy. Pretty easy!

1   POUND BABY BOK CHOY, RINSED AND TRIMMED

1   14-OUNCE CAN COCONUT MILK (SEE NOTE)

3   TABLESPOONS SHOYU OR TAMARI SOY SAUCE

¼   CUP BROWN RICE VINEGAR

½   CUP COARSELY CHOPPED CILANTRO

1   JALAPEÑO, CHOPPED

1   TABLESPOON COARSELY CHOPPED FRESH GINGER

1   GARLIC CLOVE, SLICED

2   TABLESPOONS AGAVE NECTAR

1   TEASPOON CURRY POWDER

PINCH OF CARDAMOM

PINCH OF TURMERIC

1. In a large pot of boiling water, blanch the bok choy for 30 to 40 seconds. Drain at once.

2. Place the remaining ingredients with ¼ cup of water in a blender and blend until smooth. Transfer to a saucepan and cook over low heat until warmed through. The sauce can be made ahead of time and kept, covered, in the refrigerator for up to 1 week.

3. Drizzle the sauce over the bok choy and serve at once.

NOTE: Edward and Sons "Let's Do Organic" brand makes an excellent canned coconut milk. It is available in health food stores.

SWEET AND SIMPLE SEA VEGETABLE

serves 4 as a side dish

Hiziki is a type of Japanese seaweed that's tasty on its own or when added to salads, soups, or stews. It is high in protein, calcium, phosphorus, and minerals—especially iron. Our good friend Andrea is a local macrobiotic counselor and cooking teacher and she highly recommends hiziki to promote good health.

¼ CUP HIZIKI

1 LEEK, RINSED AND THINLY SLICED ON THE DIAGONAL

1 CARROT, PEELED AND DICED

3 CELERY STALKS, DICED

1 TEASPOON SHOYU OR TAMARI SOY SAUCE

1 TEASPOON MIRIN

1 TEASPOON TOASTED SESAME OIL

2 TABLESPOONS TOASTED SUNFLOWER SEEDS

1. In a small bowl, cover the hiziki with 1 cup of water and soak until soft, about 10 to 15 minutes. Drain.

2. Transfer the hiziki and 1 cup of water to a sauté pan and cook over medium heat for 15 to 20 minutes. Add the leek, carrot, celery, shoyu or tamari soy sauce, mirin, and sesame oil and continue cooking for 5 to 7 minutes.

3. Toss the hiziki and vegetables together with the toasted sunflower seeds. Serve hot or cold.

APLE-CINNAMON SQUASH RINGLETS

serves 4 to 6 as a side dish

mad for all types of squash. Joy's mom's favorite way to prepare squash was to halve and seed butternut squash, rub it with cinnamon, then fill the cavities with chutney just before baking. We like to make something similar with sweet and succulent kabocha squash. They look and taste great as a side with grilled tofu and sautéed greens. The squash can also be cooked on the grill, basted with the maple-cinnamon mixture, about 3 minutes per side. Happy eating!

2 KABOCHA SQUASH

¼ CUP EXTRA-VIRGIN OLIVE OIL

¼ CUP MAPLE SYRUP

1 TEASPOON GROUND CINNAMON

PINCH OF CRUSHED RED PEPPER

PINCH OF SEA SALT

1. Preheat the oven to 350°F.

2. With a sharp paring or vegetable knife, carefully cut the squash into 1-inch-thick circles, then halve into semicircles. Lay them side by side on a baking sheet. In a small bowl, whisk together the olive oil, maple syrup, cinnamon, pepper, and salt. Brush the mixture over the squash rings and bake for 20 to 25 minutes, until the squash is just tender. Serve at once.

ROASTED ROOTS

serves 4 as a side dish

Look for the freshest root vegetables at the market when making this savory
and colorful dish. If you are serving a crowd, just double or triple the recipe.
Leftover roasted vegetables can be added to soups, salads, or grains.

2 MEDIUM CARROTS, PEELED AND
CUT INTO 2-INCH PIECES

2 PARSNIPS, PEELED AND CUT INTO
SMALL CHUNKS

2 BEETS, PEELED AND CUT INTO SMALL
CHUNKS

1 YAM, PEELED AND CUT INTO SMALL
CHUNKS

1 GARLIC CLOVE, SLICED

2 TABLESPOONS EXTRA-VIRGIN
OLIVE OIL

2 TABLESPOONS SHOYU OR TAMARI
SOY SAUCE

PINCH OF DRIED BASIL

PINCH OF DRIED OREGANO

PINCH OF DRIED THYME

PINCH OF FRESHLY GROUND BLACK
PEPPER

½ TEASPOON SEA SALT

HOT SAUCE (OPTIONAL)

1. Preheat the oven to 325°F.

2. In a large mixing bowl, place the carrots, parsnips, beets, yam, and garlic. Add the olive oil,
shoyu or tamari soy sauce, basil, oregano, thyme, pepper, salt, and hot sauce, if desired, to
the bowl and toss well to combine.

3. Transfer to a shallow baking sheet and bake for 45 minutes, or until tender. Taste and adjust
the seasonings. Serve warm or at room temperature.

SWEET POTATO SMASH

serves 4 to 6 as a side dish

Try these heavenly mashed sweet potatoes with hints of miso, maple syrup, and cinnamon—they're divine. We like to mash them roughly so they keep their lumpiness and texture. They are one of the Candle's most popular side dishes.

5 SWEET POTATOES	2 TEASPOONS MAPLE SYRUP
1 TABLESPOON SWEET WHITE MISO	1 TEASPOON GROUND CINNAMON

1. Preheat the oven to 350°F.

2. Bake the sweet potatoes for 45 minutes, or until tender. Cool, peel, and transfer the sweet potatoes to a large bowl. Mash them a bit with a potato masher, then add the miso, maple syrup, and cinnamon. Continue to mash until they reach the desired consistency. Serve at once.

VARIATIONS: For a savory Sweet Potato Smash, add miso with a bit of finely chopped fresh rosemary and sage leaves, omitting the syrup and cinnamon. This recipe also works well with baked parsnips, turnips, or rutabaga.

GARLIC MASHED POTATOES

serves 8 as a side dish

The Garlic Mashed Potatoes served at the Candle Cafe are wildly popular.
Our customers can't seem to get enough of them—and neither will you!

❖

6 MEDIUM YUKON GOLD POTATOES,
  PEELED AND CUT INTO ¼-INCH
  SLICES

3 GARLIC CLOVES, PEELED AND FINELY
  MINCED

3 TABLESPOONS EXTRA-VIRGIN
  OLIVE OIL

SEA SALT

FRESHLY GROUND BLACK PEPPER

½ CUP PLAIN SOY MILK (OPTIONAL)

1. In a large saucepan, place the potatoes and add enough water to cover. Bring to a boil over high heat. Reduce the heat to medium, cover, and cook until the potatoes are tender, about 20 to 25 minutes. Drain the potatoes and return them to the pot.

2. In a small bowl, mix together the garlic, oil, and salt and pepper to taste, then add them to the potatoes. Mash the potatoes with a potato masher to make a fairly smooth purée. If a creamier texture is desired, add the soy milk. Serve immediately.

VARIATIONS: For wasabi mashed potatoes, omit the garlic and add a teaspoon of wasabi paste. For rich, buttery mashed potatoes add a few tablespoons of Soy Garden or Earth's Balance buttery spread.

RED, WHITE, AND BLUE POTATOES

serves 8 to 10 as a side dish

You can make this recipe with one type of potato, or use a colorful combination of red, white, and blue potatoes. Tossed with lemon, olive oil, and herbs and roasted to perfection, this is just the right thing to serve for a festive Fourth of July barbecue. They're terrific served with Southwestern-Style Chile-Rubbed Seitan Sandwiches (page 94), Barbecued Beans (page 152), and Lemon-Caraway Slaw (page 139).

---

2 POUNDS POTATOES, SUCH AS WHITE FINGERLINGS, SMALL RED POTATOES, AND/OR BLUE POTATOES, CUT INTO 1-INCH CHUNKS

¼ CUP FRESH LEMON JUICE

⅓ CUP EXTRA-VIRGIN OLIVE OIL

¼ CUP MINCED GARLIC

¼ CUP MINCED FRESH OREGANO OR 2 TABLESPOONS DRIED OREGANO

1 TEASPOON SEA SALT

2 TEASPOONS FRESHLY GROUND BLACK PEPPER

½ CUP CHOPPED PARSLEY

1. In a large bowl, place the potatoes, lemon juice, olive oil, garlic, oregano, salt, and pepper. Toss together until the potatoes are well coated. Cover and refrigerate for several hours or, preferably, overnight.

2. Preheat the oven to 350°F.

3. Spread the potatoes in an even layer on a baking sheet and roast for 40 minutes, or until crispy and tender. Sprinkle the parsley over the potatoes and serve warm or at room temperature.

SAUTÉED MIXED GREENS

serves 6 to 8 as a side dish

Sautéed greens go well with any seitan dish and also with rice and grains.
Try this delicious combination of collard greens and kale. Feel free to add
other dark leafy greens such as spinach, watercress, or mustard greens.

---

2 TABLESPOONS EXTRA-VIRGIN
OLIVE OIL

3 GARLIC CLOVES, THINLY SLICED

½ BUNCH COLLARD GREENS, RINSED,
STEMMED, AND CHOPPED

½ BUNCH KALE, RINSED, STEMMED,
AND CHOPPED

1 TABLESPOON SOY BACON BITS
(OPTIONAL)

In a large sauté pan, heat the olive oil over medium-high heat. Add the garlic and sauté
until tender, about 2 minutes. Add the greens and sauté for another 3 minutes, until wilted
but still vibrantly green. Top with the bacon bits, if desired, and serve at once.

VARIATION: We also love steamed greens—just set greens in a steamer over
boiling water for 3 to 5 minutes.

CARAMELIZED ONIONS

serves 6 to 8 as a side dish

We serve caramelized onions over burgers and sandwiches, with seitan steak,
and in our mixed vegetable platter. They're simple but fabulous.

---

1 TEASPOON EXTRA-VIRGIN OLIVE OIL

3 ONIONS, PEELED AND THINLY SLICED

¼ TEASPOON SEA SALT

In a sauté pan heat the olive oil over medium-high heat for 30 seconds. Reduce the heat to
medium, add the onions and salt, and cook, stirring often, until the onions begin to
caramelize and turn a rich deep brown, about 15 to 20 minutes.

MINTY BARLEY PILAF

serves 6 to 8 as a side dish

Barley, a grain of the grass family, makes a deliciously chewy, nutty side dish.
Here, we cook it with vegetables, then toss it together with cashews,
fresh mint, and cilantro. This hearty but refreshing dish is a great
way to include more grains in your diet.

---

1 CUP BARLEY, RINSED AND DRAINED

½ ONION, FINELY DICED

2 SMALL CARROTS, PEELED AND
FINELY DICED

8 DRIED SHIITAKE MUSHROOMS

2 TABLESPOONS UMEBOSHI VINEGAR

¼ CUP CHOPPED CASHEWS

¼ CUP CHOPPED FRESH MINT

2 TABLESPOONS CHOPPED CILANTRO

SEA SALT AND FRESHLY GROUND
BLACK PEPPER

1. In a large saucepan, bring 4 cups of water to a boil. Add the barley, onion, carrots, and
mushrooms. Bring to a boil, then simmer, covered, for 45 minutes, or until the barley and
vegetables are tender. Remove the shiitakes with a slotted spoon, thinly slice them, then
return them to the barley mixture.

2. Add the umeboshi vinegar, cashews, mint, and cilantro and toss together. Add salt and
pepper to taste and serve at once.

WILD RICE SALAD WITH CRANBERRIES

serves 4 to 6 as a side dish

Wild rice, which is actually a seed, not a grain, is great when paired with dried fruit. The dish also works very well with diced avocados tossed into it. For those who prefer raw food, see the Note below for instructions on sprouting wild rice for your salad instead of cooking it.

1 CUP BLACK LONG-GRAIN OR OTHER WILD RICE

¼ CUP UNSALTED SUNFLOWER SEEDS, SOAKED OVERNIGHT IF DESIRED

⅓ CUP DRIED CRANBERRIES

¼ CUP CHOPPED RED ONION OR SCALLION

¼ CUP SHOYU OR TAMARI SOY SAUCE

¼ CUP FRESH LEMON JUICE

½ CUP EXTRA-VIRGIN OLIVE OIL

2 TEASPOONS GRATED ORANGE ZEST

1. Bring 1⅓ cups of water to a boil. Add the wild rice, reduce the heat, and simmer, covered, until tender, 50 to 60 minutes.

2. Transfer the rice and sunflower seeds to a large mixing bowl. Add the cranberries and onion and toss together. In another bowl, whisk together the shoyu or tamari soy sauce and lemon juice. Slowly whisk in the olive oil until well combined. Pour over the rice mixture and toss well. Sprinkle the top of the salad with the orange zest and serve at once.

NOTE: To sprout wild rice, soak the rice for 8 to 12 hours, pour off water, and resoak for another 4 to 6 hours. Drain off the water and put the rice in the refrigerator and rinse twice a day. The rice will keep for 4 to 5 days in the refrigerator.

MACROBIOTIC MILLET

serves 6 to 8 as a side dish

, which is a cereal grass, is not used often in the United States, although it is a
ary staple of Asia and Africa. Its mild taste goes well with many vegetables,
grains, and spices. Substitute cubed kabocha squash for the carrots, leeks,
and corn for a great variation on this dish.

1½ CUPS MILLET, SOAKED OVERNIGHT
AND DRAINED
PINCH OF SEA SALT
1 TABLESPOON SESAME OIL
2 CARROTS, PEELED AND MINCED

1 LEEK, RINSED AND DICED
½ CUP FRESH OR FROZEN ORGANIC
CORN KERNELS
¼ CUP TOASTED SESAME SEEDS OR
GOMASIO (PAGE 160)

1. In a large saucepan, bring 4 cups of water and salt to a boil. Add the millet and simmer for
15 minutes, until tender. Drain and transfer to a large bowl.

2. In a sauté pan over medium heat, heat the sesame oil. Add the carrots, leek, and corn and
continue cooking until the vegetables are tender, about 10 more minutes.

3. Add the cooked vegetables to the millet and toss together. Sprinkle with the sesame seeds
or Gomasio and serve warm.

BLUE CORN AND
QUINOA CORN BREAD

makes about 12 to 16 slices

Quinoa, pronounced KEEN-wah, is an amazing food. It has more protein than any
other grain and is considered a complete protein because it contains all eight
essential amino acids. It's also quite delicious. Tiny and bead-shaped, it cooks like
rice (only quicker). It's great as part of a main dish, a side dish, and in soups, salads,
or puddings. We also bake it into breads. Here's one of our favorite quinoa recipes.

QUINOA

1 TABLESPOON EXTRA-VIRGIN
  OLIVE OIL

1 CUP QUINOA, RINSED THOROUGHLY

CORN BREAD

1 CUP FRESH CORN KERNELS (FROM
  ABOUT 2 EARS OF SWEET CORN)

1 ¼ CUPS BLUE CORNMEAL

⅓ CUP SPELT FLOUR

1 TABLESPOON OAT FLOUR

1 TABLESPOON BROWN RICE FLOUR

1 ¼ TABLESPOONS BAKING POWDER

1 TEASPOON BAKING SODA

1 TEASPOON SEA SALT

1 TABLESPOON UNREFINED SUGAR

1 CUP SOY MILK

⅓ CUP MAPLE SYRUP

⅓ CUP CANOLA OIL

1 TABLESPOON FLAX EGGS
  (SEE PAGE 10)

1. To make the quinoa, heat the olive oil in a skillet. Add the quinoa and toast over high heat,
   stirring frequently, for 5 to 7 minutes. Add 2 cups of water, stir, and cover. Reduce the heat
   and simmer for 8 to 10 minutes, or until the liquid has evaporated. Set aside to cool.

2. Preheat the oven to 350°F and oil a 13 × 9 × 2-inch baking pan.

3. To make the corn bread, combine the corn, cornmeal, flours, baking powder, baking soda,
   salt, and sugar in a large mixing bowl. In a separate bowl, mix together the soy milk, maple
   syrup, oil, and flax eggs. Add the wet ingredients to the flour mixture and stir well to
   combine. Stir in the cooked quinoa. Pour the mixture into the prepared pan and bake for
   30 to 35 minutes, or until a cake tester or toothpick inserted in the center comes out clean.

BARBECUED BEANS

serves 4 to 6 as a side dish

We like to make these smoky-flavored barbecued baked beans for
summer parties to serve with grilled portobello and veggie burgers.
They're perfect for outdoor picnics and buffets, too.

---

1 CUP PINTO BEANS, RINSED AND
PICKED OVER

1 2-INCH PIECE OF KOMBU

1 CUP BARBECUE SAUCE (PAGE 162)

2 SOY HOT DOGS, CUT INTO 1-INCH
PIECES (OPTIONAL; SEE NOTE)

1. Cover the beans with water, add the kombu, and soak overnight. Rinse and drain.

2. Transfer the beans and kombu to a soup pot and cover with water by 2 inches. Bring
   to a boil, then simmer over very low heat until tender, about 1¼ hours. Add more water,
   if necessary.

3. Drain the beans, remove the kombu, then transfer the beans to a large saucepan. Add the
   Barbecue Sauce and the soy hot dogs, if using, and mix well. Cook over medium-low heat
   until heated through.

NOTE: Soy hot dogs are available at health food stores.

MARINATED GRILLED TOFU

serves 8 as a side dish

Tofu is one of today's most healthful foods—it's very low in calories and
sodium, cholesterol-free, and high in protein. Here is one of the simplest,
most versatile, and delightful recipes for tofu. It is great for salads
and sandwiches as well as vegetable and grain dishes.

¼ CUP SHOYU OR TAMARI SOY SAUCE

2 TABLESPOONS TOASTED SESAME OIL

2 TEASPOONS GRATED FRESH GINGER

2 POUNDS FIRM TOFU

1. Combine the shoyu or tamari soy sauce, sesame oil, and ginger in a jar with a tight-fitting
   lid. Shake the ingredients together until well combined. Let the marinade stand for at least
   2 hours. Any unused marinade will keep refrigerated for up to 4 weeks.

2. Prepare a gas or charcoal grill, or preheat the oven to 400°F.

3. Press any excess liquid from the tofu. Cut each block lengthwise into 3 pieces, then cut in
   half crosswise to make 6 pieces. Brush all sides of the tofu slices with the marinade.

4. Grill the tofu slices over medium-hot coals for 5 minutes on each side. If you are baking the
   tofu, place the tofu slices on a baking sheet. Bake for 15 minutes, then turn the slices over
   and continue baking for an additional 15 minutes, until golden brown.

5. Serve the grilled tofu in salads, sandwiches, and vegetable and grain dishes.

GRILLED ANCHO-CITRUS TOFU

serves 4 to 6 as a side dish

Try this tangy, Southwestern-style version of grilled tofu in a wrap,
a burrito, or a salad for a good warm-weather lunch.

———◆———

2 TOMATOES, QUARTERED

1 DRIED ANCHO CHILE, STEMMED
   AND SEEDED

2 TABLESPOONS EXTRA-VIRGIN
   OLIVE OIL

½ CUP ORANGE JUICE, PREFERABLY
   FRESH

½ CUP FRESH LIME JUICE

2 POUNDS TOFU, BLANCHED, DRAINED,
   AND CUT INTO 6 SLICES

1. Preheat the oven to 350°F.

2. Put the tomatoes and chile on a baking sheet. Drizzle with the olive oil and bake for
   20 minutes, until the tomatoes are tender. Set aside to cool.

3. Transfer the tomatoes and chile to a blender and add the orange and lime juices. Blend
   until smooth. Pour the marinade over the tofu and marinate in the refrigerator for at least
   an hour.

4. Prepare a charcoal, gas, or stovetop grill and grill the tofu, about 4 minutes per side. If you
   prefer to bake the tofu, place the tofu slices on a baking sheet. Bake for 20 minutes.

ASIAN BAKED TOFU

serves 4 as a side dish

This tofu is great in a sandwich with sunflower sprouts, snowpea shoots, and wasabi mayo, in a wrap, or with stir-fried vegetables.

———◆———

⅓ CUP SHOYU OR TAMARI SOY SAUCE

1 TABLESPOON SESAME OIL

2 TABLESPOONS MINCED FRESH GINGER

1 TABLESPOON MINCED GARLIC

¼ CUP BROWN RICE VINEGAR

2 TABLESPOONS UMEBOSHI VINEGAR

½ TEASPOON CRUSHED RED PEPPER FLAKES

1 POUND TOFU, CUT INTO 3 PIECES

1. In a bowl, whisk together ¾ cup of water, the shoyu or tamari soy sauce, oil, ginger, garlic, vinegars, and red pepper flakes and pour over the tofu. Marinate for at least an hour.

2. Preheat the oven to 375°F.

3. Drain the marinade, place the tofu on a baking sheet, and bake for 15 to 20 minutes. Turn the tofu after 10 minutes and bake for an additional 10 minutes. Serve at once.

SAUCES AND CONDIMENTS

Our creative, flavorful sauces and condiments are great accompaniments to scores of recipes throughout this book. What would our Black Bean Soup be without a dollop of tangy Tofu-Cilantro Sour Cream? Our Crystal Rolls taste even better with some Spicy Thai Dipping Sauce. Of course, our Mini Potato Latkes are delicious with a helping of Homemade Applesauce.

Many of these indispensable recipes can be made well ahead of time and stored in your refrigerator or on your kitchen shelf for several days, so you'll always have these delicious condiments on hand and ready to use at a moment's notice.

MANGO KETCHUP

makes about 2½ cups

ot your conventional ketchup from a bottle—it's a fabulous blend of fresh
toes and mangos, which we serve with burgers, sandwiches, and wraps.
This will become a mainstay in your kitchen.

———————◆———————

2 TO 3 TOMATOES, DICED

2 TABLESPOONS CHOPPED SUN-DRIED
TOMATOES, SOAKED FOR 20 MINUTES
AND DRAINED

1 MANGO, PEELED AND DICED

½ SMALL RED ONION, FINELY DICED

1 GARLIC CLOVE, MINCED

¼ CUP FINELY CHOPPED CILANTRO

1½ TEASPOONS EXTRA-VIRGIN OLIVE OIL

1½ TEASPOONS FRESH LEMON JUICE

1 JALAPEÑO PEPPER, SEEDED AND
FINELY DICED

½ TEASPOON SEA SALT

Place all of the ingredients in a blender and blend until smooth and creamy. The ketchup
will keep, covered, in the refrigerator for up to 2 weeks.

ROASTED CORN–PUMPKIN SEED RELISH

makes 6 cups

Serve as a side with almost anything. We like to make a large batch of this relish and keep it on hand since it keeps very well. This recipe is yet another gift from Angel Ramos, our chef and leader in the kitchen.

2 TABLESPOONS EXTRA-VIRGIN OLIVE OIL

3 CUPS FRESH CORN KERNELS (FROM ABOUT 6 EARS OF SWEET CORN)

1 CUP RAW, UNSALTED PUMPKIN SEEDS

1 RED ONION, DICED

4 CELERY STALKS, DICED

½ CUP CHOPPED CILANTRO

JUICE OF 2 LIMES

½ TO 1 TEASPOON CHIPOTLE PEPPER POWDER OR FINELY CHOPPED JALAPEÑO PEPPER

PINCH OF SEA SALT

1. Preheat the oven to 350°F.

2. Brush a baking sheet with the olive oil. Spread the corn on the sheet and roast for 20 minutes, or until tender.

3. Toast the pumpkin seeds in a dry skillet until they start to pop, shaking the pan often, about 3 minutes. Set aside to cool.

4. Mix the corn with the pumpkin seeds. Add the onion, celery, cilantro, lime juice, chipotle powder, and salt and stir until well combined. The relish will keep in the refrigerator, covered, for up to 2 weeks.

GOMASIO

makes 1 cup

This wonderful mixture of sesame seeds and sea salt adds flavor and
seasoning to many dishes. We fill up salt shakers with Gomasio and use
it as a topping for vegetables, salads, and grain dishes.

1 CUP RAW SESAME SEEDS   2 TEASPOONS SEA SALT

1. Toast the sesame seeds in a dry skillet over medium heat until lightly browned, being careful
   not to burn them. Set aside to cool and toss with 1 teaspoon of the sea salt.

2. Put ⅓ cup of the sesame seeds in the bowl of a food processor fitted with a steel blade.
   Process until the seeds are broken down, but not until they become sesame butter. Add the
   remaining sesame seeds and salt and mix together.

NOTE: A Japanese version of the mortar and pestle, the Suribachi and Surikogí, is a very
traditional (and aromatic) way of grinding the sesame seeds for Gomasio. They are available
at Japanese specialty markets and can be ordered from Goldmine Natural Food Company (see
Resource Guide).

SPICY THAI DIPPING SAUCE

makes 2 cups

Spicy Thai Dipping Sauce is one of our restaurant's staples. We serve it with
Crystal Rolls (page 22) as well as over soba noodles and salad greens.
Make plenty ahead of time since it keeps well in the refrigerator.

1 1/2 CUPS SMOOTH PEANUT BUTTER

1/4 CUP BROWN RICE VINEGAR OR
APPLE CIDER VINEGAR

1 SMALL RED ONION, FINELY CHOPPED

2 TABLESPOONS FINELY CHOPPED
CILANTRO

2 TABLESPOONS PEELED AND FINELY
CHOPPED FRESH GINGER

1 GARLIC CLOVE, MINCED

1/2 TEASPOON CRUSHED RED PEPPER
FLAKES

1 TABLESPOON KETCHUP

1/4 CUP SHOYU OR TAMARI SOY SAUCE

1 TABLESPOON HOT SAUCE

1/4 CUP AGAVE NECTAR

1 TABLESPOON SESAME OIL

Place all of the ingredients with 2 cups of water in a blender and blend until very smooth.
The sauce will keep in the refrigerator, covered, for up to 3 weeks. Bring to room temperature before serving.

BARBECUE SAUCE

makes about 4 cups

Our Barbecue Sauce is a pantry staple. We serve it with grilled tofu and tempeh
as well as with burgers and sandwiches. It is absolutely scrumptious!

3 DRIED OR CANNED CHIPOTLE
PEPPERS

1 CUP HOT WATER

1 TABLESPOON MINCED GARLIC

1½ CUPS TOMATO PASTE

1 CUP APPLE CIDER VINEGAR

½ CUP SHOYU OR TAMARI SOY SAUCE

½ CUP MOLASSES

1 CUP AGAVE NECTAR

¼ CUP MUSTARD

2 TEASPOONS DRIED BASIL

PINCH OF SEA SALT

FRESHLY GROUND BLACK PEPPER
TO TASTE

1. Soak the peppers in hot water for 15 minutes. Drain and discard the liquid.

2. Put the peppers and all of the remaining ingredients in a blender and blend until smooth.
Taste and adjust the seasonings, adding more molasses if you prefer a thicker, sweeter
sauce. The sauce will keep in the refrigerator, covered, for up to a week.

MARINARA SAUCE

makes about 4 cups

This is a classic sauce we use with all types of pasta and grain dishes.
It is easy to make and a good keeper. *Mangia!*

¼ CUP EXTRA-VIRGIN OLIVE OIL

4 GARLIC CLOVES, MINCED

1 ONION, COARSELY CHOPPED

1 32-OUNCE CAN ORGANIC TOMATOES,
OR 6 LARGE RED TOMATOES,
CHOPPED

¼ CUP CHOPPED FRESH BASIL

½ TEASPOON DRIED OREGANO

2 TEASPOONS DRIED ROSEMARY,
CRUMBLED

SEA SALT AND FRESHLY GROUND
BLACK PEPPER

1. In a large sauté pan or skillet, heat the olive oil over medium-high heat and sauté the garlic
   and onion until caramelized, about 5 minutes. Add the tomatoes, basil, oregano, and rosemary and cook over medium-low heat for 20 minutes, stirring occasionally. Remove from the
   heat and let cool. Add salt and pepper to taste.

2. Transfer the mixture to a blender and blend until smooth. This may have to be done in
   batches. The sauce will keep in the refrigerator, covered, for up to a week. It can be frozen
   for a month. Reheat before serving.

VARIATION: For a vegan Bolognese sauce, sauté chopped seitan or tempeh until
browned, then stir into the finished sauce. Great for lasagna or over pasta!

B-12 TAMARI DIJON

makes about 3 cups

We use our vitamin-rich tamari dijon as a dipping sauce for dumplings and as an accompaniment to rice, grains, and salads. Our customers love it and protested loudly when we temporarily took it off the menu a few years ago.

1 CUP SHOYU OR WHEAT-FREE TAMARI

1 CUP NUTRITIONAL YEAST FLAKES

2 TABLESPOONS DIJON MUSTARD

2 TABLESPOONS DRIED BASIL

1 TABLESPOON DRIED PARSLEY

1 TABLESPOON BROWN RICE SYRUP

Place all of the ingredients with 2 cups of water in a blender and blend for about 30 seconds. The sauce will keep in the refrigerator, covered, for at least a week. Bring to room temperature and shake well before serving.

UNIVERSAL MARINADE

makes 2 cups

Our tangy, herb-infused Universal Marinade is very versatile. We use it for raw foods that require overnight marinating, as well as in numerous vegetable, salad, and grill recipes, including Spicy Soba Noodle Stir-Fry (page 124).

½ CUP APPLE CIDER VINEGAR

½ CUP EXTRA-VIRGIN OLIVE OIL

1 SMALL RED ONION, FINELY CHOPPED

1 TABLESPOON FINELY CHOPPED FRESH BASIL OR ½ TABLESPOON DRIED BASIL

¼ CUP SHOYU OR TAMARI SOY SAUCE

½ CUP FRESH LEMON JUICE

PINCH OF SEA SALT

FRESHLY GROUND BLACK PEPPER

Put all of the ingredients in a blender and blend until smooth. The marinade will keep in the refrigerator, covered, for up to 5 days.

WILD MUSHROOM GRAV

makes about 4 cups

Flavorful Wild Mushroom Gravy is a wonderful accompaniment to Homemade
Steaks (page 117) and many vegetables, including Stuffed Winter Squash (pag

6 TABLESPOONS EXTRA-VIRGIN
OLIVE OIL

2 CUPS ONION, PEELED AND FINELY
CHOPPED

2 CUPS FINELY CHOPPED MUSHROOMS,
SUCH AS SHIITAKE, OYSTER,
CHANTERELLE, OR PORTOBELLO

1 CUP BROWN RICE FLOUR

½ CUP SHOYU OR TAMARI SOY SAUCE

1 ½ TEASPOONS DRIED SAGE

1 ½ TEASPOONS DRIED ROSEMARY

1 ½ TEASPOONS DRIED TARRAGON

1. Heat 3 tablespoons of the olive oil in a large skillet. Sauté the onion and mushrooms until softened, about 10 minutes, and set aside.

2. In a medium saucepan, heat the remaining 3 tablespoons of olive oil and sauté the rice flour over low heat to make a roux. Stir 2 cups of water, the shoyu or tamari soy sauce, sage, rosemary, and tarragon into the roux and mix well. Bring to a boil over medium heat, then simmer until the gravy is thickened and smooth, about 10 minutes.

3. Stir in the mushroom-onion mixture and cook over low heat until warmed through. If the gravy is too thick, add water 1 tablespoon at a time to achieve the right consistency. Serve at once.

VEGAN MAYO

makes about 3 cups

Homemade Vegan Mayo is much better and fresher-tasting than store-bought.
We use it so many ways—on sandwiches, including our famous Tofu Club Sandwiches
on Multi-Grain Toast (page 92) and spread on burgers and wraps.
Try all of the variations—they're great.

1 CUP SOY MILK

2½ CUPS SAFFLOWER OIL

1½ TABLESPOONS CIDER VINEGAR

¼ TEASPOON DRY MUSTARD

1 TABLESPOON AGAVE NECTAR

DASH OF HOT SAUCE

1 TABLESPOON SEA SALT

FRESHLY GROUND BLACK PEPPER

Place the soy milk in a blender and, with the blender still running, slowly drizzle in the oil. Continue adding the oil until it is all absorbed. Transfer to a large bowl and whisk in the vinegar, mustard, agave nectar, hot sauce, salt, and pepper to taste. The mayo will keep in the refrigerator, covered, for up to a week.

VARIATIONS: To make spicy Chipotle Mayo, whisk ¼ cup plus 2 tablespoons cider vinegar into 3 cups Vegan Mayo. Add 1 tablespoon chipotle chile powder and 1 teaspoon paprika.

To make Cajun Mayo, whisk 1 tablespoon paprika, 1½ teaspoons each chopped garlic, dried thyme, and onion powder, and a pinch each of cayenne, sea salt, and freshly ground black and white pepper into 3 cups Vegan Mayo.

To make Wasabi Mayo, add 3 tablespoons wasabi powder to 3 cups Vegan Mayo.

TOFU-CILANTRO SOUR CREAM

makes about 3 cups

This is a delicious garnish for soups and it's also great on baked potatoes or Mexican dishes. You can make it with other fresh herbs, such as parsley, basil, or chives, mixed together or on their own.

---

2 TEASPOONS AGAR-AGAR POWDER (OPTIONAL)

4 TABLESPOONS FRESH LEMON JUICE

2 TABLESPOONS FRESH LIME JUICE

1 POUND FIRM TOFU

⅓ CUP EXTRA-VIRGIN OLIVE OIL

2 TABLESPOONS SAFFLOWER OIL

¼ CUP CHOPPED CILANTRO

1½ TEASPOONS SEA SALT

¼ TEASPOON CAYENNE

½ TEASPOON MINCED GARLIC

1. In a nonreactive bowl, dissolve the agar in the lemon and lime juice.

2. Blanch the tofu for 5 minutes, drain, and allow to cool for 20 minutes. Crumble the tofu and transfer to a blender.

3. Add the remaining ingredients and blend until smooth. The sour cream will keep in the refrigerator, covered, for up to 3 days.

SALSA VERDE

makes about 2 cups

The slightly tart tomatillos and lime in our Salsa Verde blend beautifully with
spicy onions and jalapeños. Use it as a dip for tortilla chips, or to add a spicy kick
to salads, wraps, and more. For a great variation, add a chopped avocado
just before you've finished blending the sauce.

5 TO 6 TOMATILLOS, HUSKED

2 TABLESPOONS EXTRA-VIRGIN
   OLIVE OIL

   JUICE OF 1 LIME

½ RED ONION, FINELY CHOPPED

1 TO 2 JALAPEÑO PEPPERS, SEEDED
   AND DICED

½ BUNCH OF CILANTRO, CHOPPED

1 TEASPOON SEA SALT (OPTIONAL)

1. Preheat the oven to 350°F.

2. Lightly coat the tomatillos in the olive oil. Place them in a baking dish and sprinkle with
   lime juice. Bake for 30 minutes. Remove and let cool.

3. Transfer the tomatillos to a blender and add the onion, peppers, cilantro, and salt, if
   desired. Blend just until chunky. The sauce will keep in the refrigerator, covered, for up
   to 5 days.

MISO PESTO

makes about 2 cups

This is a versatile pesto spread that can be used in many delicious ways.
We like to spread it on grilled vegetable sandwiches and on crostini with
slices of grilled portobello mushrooms, or toss it with freshly cooked pasta.
You can make it with spinach or basil, or a combination of both.

3 CUPS FRESH SPINACH OR BASIL,
RINSED AND PATTED DRY

2 GARLIC CLOVES

¼ CUP EXTRA-VIRGIN OLIVE OIL

¼ CUP WALNUTS OR PINE NUTS

1 TABLESPOON SWEET WHITE MISO

Place all the ingredients in a food processor fitted with a steel blade and blend until smooth. The pesto will keep in the refrigerator, covered, for up to 2 days. Bring to room temperature before serving.

HOMEMADE APPLESAUCE

makes about 6 cups

Applesauce made from freshly picked apples is homey and delicious. We cook our
version with unpeeled organic apples because the flavor from the skins is so sweet
and intense. Served as an accompaniment to Mini Potato Latkes (page 10)
or over pancakes or French toast, it's always a welcome treat.

---

1 DOZEN TART APPLES, SUCH AS
GRANNY SMITH, STEMMED AND
QUARTERED

½–1 CUP UNREFINED SUGAR

2 TABLESPOONS FRESH LEMON JUICE

1½ TABLESPOONS GROUND CINNAMON

¼ TEASPOON GRATED NUTMEG,
PREFERABLY FRESHLY GRATED

1. Place the apples and 3 cups of water in a large pan, cover, and cook over low heat for
   30 minutes. Add the sugar, lemon juice, cinnamon, and nutmeg and cook, uncovered,
   for an additional 30 minutes. Stir the applesauce frequently, mashing with the back of a
   wooden spoon. Remove from the heat and set aside to cool.

2. Strain the applesauce. Taste and adjust the seasonings. The applesauce can be served
   warm, cold, or at room temperature.

HANDMADE CROUTONS

makes about 2 cups

Freshly made croutons are an excellent addition to all types of soups and salads. We use them in many of our classic dishes, such as Caesar Salad (page 66) and Onion Soup (page 58). The variations made with corn bread and herbs are also excellent.

¼ CUP EXTRA-VIRGIN OLIVE OIL

SEA SALT AND FRESHLY GROUND
BLACK PEPPER

2 CUPS DAY-OLD 1-INCH BREAD CUBES

Preheat the oven to 350°F. In a large bowl, whisk together the olive oil and salt and pepper to taste. Toss the bread cubes with the olive oil mixture until well coated. Add salt and pepper to taste. Place in a single layer on a baking sheet and bake until golden brown, 15 to 20 minutes. Remove and set aside to cool.

VARIATIONS: To make Herbed Croutons, add ½ teaspoon dried thyme and ½ teaspoon dried oregano to the olive oil before tossing with the bread. These are very good in salads.

To make Corn Bread Croutons, toss 2 cups of day-old corn bread cubes with the olive oil, salt, and pepper. They are delicious as a garnish for Butternut Squash Soup (page 51) and other creamy soups.

DESSERTS

Our customers, vegetarian and nonvegetarian alike, are always amazed at our range of delicious but wholesome desserts. We use no dairy products or refined sugars in our baking. Instead, organic ingredients such as silken and firm tofu, soy milk, and soy margarine give our desserts their great reputation. Whole wheat, brown rice, unbleached white, and wheat-free spelt flours are baked into our cakes, piecrusts, and cookies. For sweeteners we use unrefined sugar and agave nectar, as well as maple syrup and natural fruit juices—so much more flavorful than plain sugar. All of these ingredients are available at health food stores and through mail-order outlets—see the Resource Guide for more information.

The Candle Cafe is famous for its desserts, so rest assured you and your guests will enjoy every last bite.

LEMON-TOFU CHEESECAKE WITH BLOOD ORANGE GLAZE

makes one 9-inch cheesecake, serves 8

This light and lovely cheesecake always wins raves. The crust, filling, and glaze are flavored with agave nectar, a honeylike sweet syrup that comes from a succulent plant indigenous to the Southwest and Mexico. Also called *century plant*, certain varieties of agave are used in making tequila. We make the glaze with sweet-tart blood oranges, but it can also be made with navel oranges. The cheesecake should be made ahead of time to allow it to chill for at least 12 hours.

CRUST

2 CUPS SPELT FLOUR

¼ CUP PLUS 2 TABLESPOONS AGAVE NECTAR

¼ CUP SAFFLOWER OIL

FILLING

1 CUP FRESH LEMON JUICE (ABOUT 6 LEMONS)

1 TABLESPOON LEMON EXTRACT

3 CUPS DAIRY-FREE TOFU CREAM CHEESE

½ CUP ARROWROOT POWDER

4½ TEASPOONS AGAR-AGAR POWDER

2 CUPS AGAVE NECTAR

½ TABLESPOON TURMERIC

GLAZE

2 TABLESPOONS ARROWROOT POWDER

1 CUP APPLE JUICE

½ CUP FRESH BLOOD ORANGE JUICE (ABOUT 2 ORANGES)

2 TABLESPOONS AGAVE NECTAR

1. To make the crust, preheat the oven to 325°F. In a large bowl, mix together the flour, agave nectar, and oil. Flatten the mixture out on a large baking sheet and bake for 15 minutes, or until golden. Remove from the oven and set aside to cool.

2. Put the mixture in a food processor or blender and process until smooth. This may have to be done in batches.

3. Using your fingers, press the baked crust crumbs evenly into the bottom of a 9-inch spring-form pan, adding a bit of water if the mixture is too dry. Wrap the bottom and sides of the pan in tinfoil.

4. To make the filling, place the lemon juice, lemon extract, tofu cream cheese, arrowroot, agar-agar, agave nectar, and turmeric in a blender and blend until smooth. Pour the mixture into the prepared crust. Place the pan in a larger ovenproof pan and fill the larger pan with enough boiling water to reach halfway up the side of the smaller pan. Place in the oven and bake for 55 minutes, or until the cake is set. When the cake is cool, chill in the refrigerator overnight.

5. To make the blood orange glaze, dissolve the arrowroot in ½ cup of the apple juice and set aside. Place the orange juice, agave nectar, and the remaining apple juice in a medium saucepan and bring to a boil over medium heat. When the fruit juice mixture just begins to boil, add the arrowroot and apple juice mixture, stirring constantly, until thickened and smooth, about 10 to 15 minutes. Chill the sauce in the refrigerator for at least 1 hour.

6. To assemble the cake, unmold the cake from the springform pan onto a serving dish and top with the blood orange glaze. Serve chilled or at room temperature.

CHOCOLATE CAKE WITH CHOCOLATE GANACHE FROSTING

makes one 9-inch layer cake, serves 8 to 10

This decadent and delicious cake has been a big part of many celebrations
at the Candle. We've made it for numerous birthday, anniversary, and holiday
parties for our friends and families. People who bake with eggs and
dairy products are amazed that this is a totally dairy-free recipe.

---

1 CUP UNBLEACHED WHITE FLOUR

1 CUP PASTRY FLOUR

2 TEASPOONS BAKING POWDER

2 TEASPOONS BAKING SODA

½ CUP UNSWEETENED COCOA POWDER

1 TEASPOON SEA SALT (FINE-GRAINED)

½ TEASPOON GROUND CINNAMON

½ CUP UNREFINED SUGAR

1 CUP SOY MILK

1 CUP MAPLE SYRUP

½ CUP SAFFLOWER OIL

2 TEASPOONS APPLE CIDER VINEGAR

1 TEASPOON VANILLA EXTRACT

½ TEASPOON ALMOND EXTRACT

CHOCOLATE GANACHE FROSTING

4 CUPS DAIRY-FREE CHOCOLATE CHIPS

1 CUP VANILLA SOY MILK

1 TABLESPOON BREWED COFFEE

¼ CUP MAPLE SYRUP OR AGAVE NECTAR

1. Preheat the oven to 350°F.

2. In a large mixing bowl, mix together the flours, baking powder, baking soda, cocoa
powder, salt, cinnamon, and sugar. In another bowl, mix together ½ cup of water, the soy
milk, maple syrup, oil, vinegar, and vanilla and almond extracts. Pour the wet ingredients
into the flour mixture and stir well to combine.

3. Divide the batter into 2 greased 9-inch cake pans. Bake for 35 minutes, or until a cake tester
or toothpick comes out clean when inserted into the center of the cake. Remove from the
oven and let cool on wire racks for about 30 minutes.

4. To prepare the frosting, put the chocolate chips, soy milk, coffee, and maple syrup or agave
nectar in a double boiler over simmering water. Once the chips are melted, remove from
the double boiler and set aside to cool. Transfer the mixture to a blender and blend for
1 minute. Cool for about an hour in the refrigerator.

5. Place one cake layer on a plate and frost about ½ inch thick. Place the second cake layer
on top and frost the entire cake.

NOTE: If you have any frosting left over, it can be stored in the refrigerator for up to a
week. Use as a topping for ice cream and other desserts.

CARROT CAKE WITH TOFU CREAM CHEESE FROSTING

makes one 9-inch layer cake, serves 8 to 10

This cake is sugar and spice and everything nice. It's a lovely treat to
savor in the afternoon with a cup of tea.

1 CUP UNBLEACHED FLOUR

1 CUP PASTRY FLOUR

1 TEASPOON BAKING POWDER

1 TEASPOON BAKING SODA

2 TEASPOONS GROUND CINNAMON

1/2 TEASPOON SEA SALT (FINE-GRAINED)

1/2 TEASPOON GRATED NUTMEG

1/2 TEASPOON GROUND CLOVES

1/2 CUP SOY MILK

1 CUP MAPLE SYRUP

1/4 CUP SAFFLOWER OIL

1 TEASPOON VANILLA EXTRACT

2 CUPS SHREDDED CARROTS

1/2 CUP RAISINS

1/2 CUP CHOPPED FRESH PINEAPPLE

CREAM CHEESE FROSTING

1/2 BLOCK (8 OUNCES) SILKEN TOFU

1/2 CUP UNREFINED SUGAR

2 TABLESPOONS SAFFLOWER OIL OR
SPECTRUM SPREAD

1 1/2 CUPS TOFUTTI CREAM CHEESE
(TOFUTTI BRAND)

1. Preheat the oven to 325°F. Grease two 9-inch round cake pans.

2. In a large mixing bowl, mix together the flours, baking powder, baking soda, cinnamon, salt, nutmeg, and cloves. In another bowl, combine the soy milk, maple syrup, oil, and vanilla extract. Pour the wet ingredients into the flour mixture and stir well to combine. Mix in the carrots, raisins, and pineapple.

3. Divide the batter into the 2 prepared cake pans. Bake for 35 minutes, or until a cake tester or toothpick comes out clean when inserted into the center of the cake. Remove from the oven and let cool on wire racks for about 30 minutes.

4. To prepare the frosting, bring 4 cups of water to a boil in a large saucepan and add the tofu. Cook for 5 minutes, then remove the tofu and put in a bowl of cold water. Remove the tofu and squeeze it to remove any excess water. Transfer to a blender or food processor, add the sugar, oil or Spectrum Spread, and cream cheese. Process until smooth, about 2 minutes. Chill for at least 20 minutes.

5. Place one cake layer on a plate and spread a 1/4-inch-thick layer of frosting over it. Place the second cake layer on top and frost the entire cake.

BLACK AND WHITE CUPCAKES

makes 12 cupcakes

Black and white cookies are found in almost every deli in New York.
Our Black and White Cupcakes are even more luscious. They're always
a big winner with kids and great for treats at school or for birthday parties.

---

1 CUP WHOLE WHEAT FLOUR

1 CUP UNBLEACHED FLOUR

¼ CUP UNREFINED SUGAR

1 TEASPOON BAKING SODA

1 TEASPOON BAKING POWDER

½ TEASPOON SEA SALT (FINE-GRAINED)

¼ CUP SAFFLOWER OIL

1 CUP MAPLE SYRUP

1 CUP SOY MILK

1 TEASPOON APPLE CIDER VINEGAR

BLACK AND WHITE FROSTING

½ BLOCK FIRM TOFU

½ CUP SPECTRUM SPREAD, COCONUT BUTTER, OR SOY MARGARINE (SEE NOTE)

½ CUP UNREFINED SUGAR

2 CUPS TOFUTTI CREAM CHEESE

½ CUP UNSWEETENED COCOA POWDER

1. Preheat the oven to 350°F. Grease a muffin pan or line one with cupcake papers.

2. Sift the flours, sugar, baking soda, baking powder, and salt into a medium bowl and whisk to mix. Put the oil, maple syrup, soy milk, and vinegar into another bowl and whisk until foamy. Pour the wet ingredients into the flour mixture and mix until the batter is smooth. Pour the batter into the prepared muffin pans, dividing evenly.

3. Bake the cupcakes on the center rack of the oven for 20 to 25 minutes. Let cool slightly and carefully remove the cupcakes from the pan.

4. To make the frosting, boil the tofu for 20 minutes, remove from the water with a strainer, and let cool for about 20 minutes. Place the tofu between sheets of paper towels and squeeze out the excess water. Crumble the tofu and transfer to a food processor (or use a hand mixer). Add the Spectrum Spread and sugar and mix for 3 to 5 minutes, or until well blended. Add the cream cheese and continue to mix for about a minute, until very creamy. Transfer half of the frosting to a separate bowl and stir in the cocoa powder.

5. Frost half of each cupcake top with the vanilla frosting and the other half with the chocolate frosting.

NOTE: Soy Garden, a vegan butter spread, and Coconut Butter are excellent alternatives to butter. Earth Balance, Spectrum Spread, and Willow Run are very good brands of vegan margarine. They are available in health food stores and can also be bought online.

APPLE PIE

makes one 8-inch pie, serves 6 to 8

We look for the freshest, most tart apples to make our simple and homey apple pies
and we've found that Granny Smith, Jonathan, or Northern Spy varieties
work best. Be sure to chill the safflower oil or coconut butter before
making the piecrust to ensure flakiness.

PIECRUST

- 1 CUP WHOLE WHEAT PASTRY FLOUR
- 1 CUP UNBLEACHED FLOUR
- ½ TEASPOON GROUND CINNAMON
- PINCH OF SEA SALT (FINE-GRAINED)
- ⅓ CUP COLD SAFFLOWER OIL OR COCONUT BUTTER
- ⅓ CUP ICE WATER

FILLING

- 4 CUPS TART APPLES, SUCH AS GRANNY SMITH, JONATHAN, OR NORTHERN SPY, PEELED, CORED, AND SLICED ABOUT ¼ INCH THICK
- 3 TABLESPOONS MAPLE SYRUP
- 1 TEASPOON FRESH LEMON JUICE
- 1 TABLESPOON UNBLEACHED FLOUR
- 1 TEASPOON GROUND CINNAMON
- ¼ TEASPOON GRATED NUTMEG

1. Sift the flours, cinnamon, and salt into a medium bowl. Add the oil and mix well. Add the ice water gradually to the mixture while continuing to mix the dough. Continue to mix until the dough is firm but not flaky. Roll up the dough, put into a bowl, and let it rest in the refrigerator for 30 minutes. Form the dough into 2 balls. Roll one out into a circle with a ½-inch thickness. Press into an 8-inch pie pan and trim, leaving ½ inch all around.

2. Preheat the oven to 350°F.

3. In a large bowl, combine the apples, maple syrup, and lemon juice. In a small bowl, mix together the flour, cinnamon, and nutmeg, then toss with the apple mixture. Add the filling into the pie shell. Roll out the second ball of dough into a circle large enough to cover the pie. Top the pie with the dough, then trim any excess and crimp the edges. Cut 3 slits in the top crust.

4. Bake for 1½ hours, or until the piecrust is golden.

STRAWBERRY-RHUBARB CRUMB PIE

makes one 8-inch pie, serves 6 to 8

This is a delicious summer treat to be served when strawberries and rhubarb are at their luscious peak. This recipe also adapts very well to other fruit combinations, such as blueberries and peaches. It's great served à la mode with vanilla soy ice cream.

PIECRUST

- 1 CUP WHOLE WHEAT PASTRY FLOUR
- 1 CUP UNBLEACHED FLOUR
- PINCH OF SEA SALT (FINE-GRAINED)
- ½ TEASPOON GROUND CINNAMON
- ⅓ CUP COLD SAFFLOWER OIL OR COCONUT BUTTER
- ⅓ CUP ICE WATER

FILLING

- 1 CUP CUBED RHUBARB (ABOUT 2 LARGE STALKS)
- 1 QUART STRAWBERRIES, HALVED
- ¼ CUP UNREFINED SUGAR
- 2 TABLESPOONS ARROWROOT POWDER
- ½ TEASPOON GROUND CINNAMON
- 1 TABLESPOON SAFFLOWER OIL OR SPECTRUM SPREAD

CRUMB TOPPING

- ⅔ CUP ROLLED OATS
- ½ CUP CHOPPED WALNUTS
- ⅓ CUP UNREFINED SUGAR
- PINCH OF SEA SALT (FINE-GRAINED)
- ¼ TEASPOON GROUND CINNAMON
- 1 CUP UNBLEACHED FLOUR
- ¼ CUP SAFFLOWER OIL

1. Sift the flours, salt, and cinnamon into a medium bowl. Add the oil, stir to combine, and mix well. Add the ice water to the mixture gradually while continuing to mix the dough until it is firm but not flaky. Roll up the dough into a ball and place in the refrigerator for 30 minutes. Roll the dough out into a circle with ⅓-inch thickness. Press into an 8-inch pie pan and trim, leaving ½ inch all around. Fold the edge under and then crimp.

2. Preheat the oven to 325°F.

3. In a large bowl, combine the rhubarb, strawberries, sugar, arrowroot, cinnamon, and oil and toss well.

4. Place the oats, nuts, sugar, salt, and cinnamon in a food processor and process until very finely ground. Add the flour and continue to mix in the food processor. Add the safflower oil and continue to mix, making sure the mixture remains firm. If it becomes too dry or crumbly, slowly add a little more water. The topping can be stored in the refrigerator for up to 5 days.

5. Pour the filling into the piecrust, then top with the crumb topping. Bake for 45 minutes.

COCONUT ALMOND JOY

serves 6 to 8

We like to make this cold, refreshing, mousselike dessert well ahead of time
and serve it for a dinner party the next evening. It's delicious made with soy
or almond milk, or a combination of both, and topped with fruit like
strawberries, blueberries, mangos, or apricots.

---

2 CUPS SOY OR ALMOND MILK

1 8-OUNCE PACKAGE SILKEN TOFU

1 ⅓ CUPS AGAVE NECTAR

½ CUP ARROWROOT POWDER

1 TABLESPOON AGAR-AGAR POWDER

3 CUPS UNSWEETENED SHREDDED
COCONUT

⅓ CUP TOASTED UNSWEETENED
GRATED FRESH COCONUT (SEE NOTE)

½ CUP TOASTED SLIVERED ALMONDS
(SEE NOTE)

SEASONAL FRESH FRUIT OF CHOICE,
FOR GARNISH (OPTIONAL)

1. Grease a 13 × 9 × 2-inch baking pan.

2. In a saucepan, put the soy or almond milk, tofu, agave nectar, arrowroot powder, agar-
agar, and 2 cups of the coconut and stir to combine. Cook over medium heat, stirring
frequently, until thickened and smooth, 10 to 15 minutes. Remove from the heat and cool.
Fold the remaining cup of coconut into the soy mixture.

3. Slowly pour the mixture evenly into the greased baking pan. Top with the toasted coconut
and let cool in the refrigerator overnight, making sure the mixture is completely set before
serving. Cut into squares, sprinkle with toasted almonds, garnish with fruit, if desired, and
serve.

NOTE: To toast the coconut, preheat the oven to 350°F. Spread the coconut on a baking
sheet and bake until lightly browned, about 3 minutes.

To toast the almonds, spread them on a baking sheet and toast them in a preheated 350°F
oven for about 5 minutes, or until golden brown. Shake the pan once or twice midway for even
toasting. Slide the nuts off the baking sheet to stop the cooking.

VARIATION: This is also great drizzled with melted chocolate or heated fat-free
fudge sauce.

CHOCOLATE MOUSSE PIE

makes one 9-inch pie, serves 6 to 8

This rich-tasting, luxurious Chocolate Mousse Pie is great for chocoholics. For an excellent variation, make it with a combination of chocolate and peanut butter chips.

PIECRUST

- 1 CUP SPELT FLOUR
- ¼ CUP UNSWEETENED COCOA POWDER
- ¼ CUP UNREFINED SUGAR
- 1 TEASPOON BAKING POWDER
- 1 TEASPOON BAKING SODA
- ½ CUP SOY MILK
- ½ CUP MAPLE SYRUP
- ¼ CUP SAFFLOWER OIL
- ½ TEASPOON VANILLA EXTRACT
- ¼ TEASPOON ALMOND EXTRACT
- 2 TABLESPOONS DAIRY-FREE CHOCOLATE CHIPS

MOUSSE

- 2¼ CUPS DAIRY-FREE CHOCOLATE CHIPS
- 1 CUP PLUS 2 TABLESPOONS VANILLA SOY MILK
- ½ TEASPOON UNSWEETENED COCOA POWDER
- ½ TEASPOON KUZU
- 1¼ BLOCKS (20 OUNCES) SILKEN TOFU
- ¼ CUP MAPLE SYRUP
- 2 TEASPOONS VANILLA EXTRACT
- ½ TEASPOON ALMOND EXTRACT

1. To prepare the piecrust, preheat the oven to 325°F.

2. In a large mixing bowl, mix together the flour, cocoa powder, sugar, baking powder, and baking soda. In another bowl, combine the soy milk, maple syrup, oil, ½ cup of water, and the vanilla and almond extracts. Add the wet ingredients to the flour mixture and stir well to combine. Pour the mixture into a baking pan and bake for 35 minutes. Let cool in the refrigerator for about an hour.

3. Crumble the baked dough and press the crust crumbs into a 9-inch pie plate. Sprinkle the crust with the 2 tablespoons of chocolate chips.

4. To prepare the mousse filling, place the chocolate chips, 1 cup of soy milk, and the cocoa powder in a bowl. Dissolve the kuzu in the remaining 2 tablespoons of soy milk and add to the mixture. Place the mixture in a double boiler and heat over simmering water on medium heat until melted, stirring occasionally, 15 to 20 minutes. Transfer to a mixing bowl and let cool slightly.

5. Place the tofu in a blender and blend until smooth. Add the maple syrup and vanilla and almond extracts and blend again. Fold into the chocolate mixture until well blended.

6. Pour the chocolate mixture into the piecrust and chill up to 2 hours or overnight before serving.

TIRAMISÙ

serves 12 to 14

Tiramisù, loosely translated as "pick me up," is a wildly popular Italian dessert. Try our light and delicious vegan version, made with tofu cream cheese and natural sweeteners.

SPONGE CAKE

- 1 CUP WHOLE WHEAT PASTRY FLOUR
- 1 CUP UNBLEACHED WHITE FLOUR
- 1 TABLESPOON BAKING POWDER
- ¼ CUP UNREFINED SUGAR
- ¼ TEASPOON GROUND CINNAMON
- ¼ TEASPOON SEA SALT (FINE-GRAINED)
- 1 CUP VANILLA SOY MILK
- ¾ CUP MAPLE SYRUP
- ¼ CUP EGG REPLACER
- 2 TABLESPOONS SAFFLOWER OIL
- ½ TEASPOON VANILLA EXTRACT

VEGAN CREAM CHEESE FILLING

- ¾ CUP TOFU CREAM CHEESE
- 12 OUNCES SILKEN TOFU
- ½ CUP MAPLE SYRUP
- ½ CUP UNREFINED SUGAR
- 1 ½ TEASPOONS AGAR-AGAR POWDER
- ½ CUP BREWED ESPRESSO
- ¼ TEASPOON GROUND CINNAMON
- 2 TABLESPOONS UNSWEETENED COCOA POWDER

1. Preheat the oven to 350°F. Grease a 13 × 9 × 2-inch baking pan.

2. In a large bowl, combine the flours, baking powder, unrefined sugar, cinnamon, and sea salt. In another bowl, mix the soy milk, maple syrup, egg replacer, oil, and vanilla together and add to the flour mixture. Spread in the greased baking pan and bake for 10 to 15 minutes.

3. Put the cream cheese, tofu, maple syrup, unrefined sugar, ¼ cup of water, and the agar-agar in a food processor and process until smooth. Cook in a saucepan for 5 minutes, until heated through. Refrigerate for 10 minutes.

4. Cut the cake in half horizontally and place the bottom half in a pan large enough to fit the halved sponge cake snugly. Moisten the cake with half of the espresso. Top with half of the cream cheese mixture. Sprinkle with the cinnamon and cocoa powder. Place the other half of the cake on top of that mixture, pour the remaining espresso on the cake, and then spread the remaining cream mixture evenly over the cake. Sprinkle with the remaining cinnamon and cocoa. Refrigerate for at least 2 hours before serving. Slice into squares and serve chilled.

MANGO-BLUEBERRY TORTE

makes one 9-inch torte, serves 6 to 8

You, your family, and your guests will flip over this dessert! There is no cooking involved, it's packed full of nutrients, and it tastes fantastic! Chef Renée Loux Underkoffler made this with us in our kitchen to serve at the PETA event at the Waldorf-Astoria and it impressed all of the attendees. Thank you, Renée, for sharing your recipe and your love!

CRUST

1 ½ CUPS PECANS

6 LARGE SOFT DATES, PITTED AND CHOPPED

1 TABLESPOON GROUND CINNAMON

1 TEASPOON GRATED NUTMEG, PREFERABLY FRESHLY GRATED

PINCH OF SEA SALT (FINE-GRAINED)

VANILLA BEAN AND COCONUT CREAM

½ CUP DRIED SHREDDED COCONUT

1 VANILLA BEAN, SPLIT, INSIDE SCRAPED

½ CUP COCONUT MILK

1 TABLESPOON VANILLA EXTRACT

4 TO 6 TABLESPOONS DATE SUGAR OR OTHER UNREFINED SUGAR

1 FIRM, RIPE MANGO, PEELED, PITTED, AND THINLY SLICED

1 PINT FRESH OR FROZEN BLUEBERRIES

1. Soak the pecans for 6 to 8 hours, rinse, drain, and dry well with a towel.

2. Place the pecans in a food processor and process into a meal. Add the dates, cinnamon, nutmeg, and salt and process until thoroughly mixed. Press into a 9-inch torte pan or pie plate.

3. In a food processor, grind the dried shredded coconut into a powder. Scrape to loosen the vanilla seeds from the vanilla bean into the food processor, add the coconut milk, vanilla extract, and date sugar and blend until smooth, adding a few tablespoons of water, if necessary.

4. Mix the mango slices with the coconut cream and smooth into the piecrust. Generously cover with blueberries and chill for an hour to set.

BROWN RICE PUDDING

serves 8 to 10

This is good comfort food. It's filling and nourishing and lovely to have for breakfast, as well as for a late-night dessert. We like to top it with all kinds of good things, like blueberries, toasted almonds, or maple syrup.

---

1 ½ CUPS BROWN RICE

2 TABLESPOONS ARROWROOT POWDER

1 ½ CUPS VANILLA SOY MILK OR ANY NUT MILK

¼ CUP RAISINS

¼ CUP MAPLE SYRUP

1 TABLESPOON GROUND CINNAMON

½ TEASPOON SEA SALT (FINE-GRAINED)

1. Preheat the oven to 350°F. Bring the brown rice and 3 cups of water to a boil in a heavy medium saucepan. Reduce the heat to low, cover, and simmer for 40 to 50 minutes, or until very soft.

2. In a large bowl, dissolve the arrowroot powder in 1 cup of the soy milk. Then add the rice, raisins, maple syrup, cinnamon, and salt and mix well to combine. Transfer to a large greased baking dish, cover with foil, and bake for 1 hour, or until lightly browned and bubbly.

3. Remove from the oven and stir in the remaining ½ cup of soy milk. Let cool for about 1 hour before serving.

VARIATIONS: For a fruity version, stir dried blueberries, cherries, or apricots into the baked pudding. Add nuts for a crunchy accent.

PUMPKIN PUDDING

serves 6 to 8

Serve this nice and easy pudding for dessert on a cold winter's night. It's also a good taste treat for the holidays, garnished with vanilla ice cream and mint.

½ CUP ARROWROOT POWDER OR KUZU

4 CUPS VANILLA SOY MILK

3 CUPS CANNED PUMPKIN PURÉE, PREFERABLY ORGANIC

½ CUP MAPLE SYRUP

1 TEASPOON GROUND CINNAMON

½ TEASPOON SEA SALT (FINE-GRAINED)

VANILLA SOY ICE CREAM OR TOFU WHIP, FOR GARNISH (OPTIONAL)

MINT LEAVES, FOR GARNISH (OPTIONAL)

1. Preheat the oven to 350°F.

2. In a large mixing bowl, dissolve the arrowroot powder in the soy milk. Add the pumpkin purée, maple syrup, cinnamon, and salt and mix well to combine. Transfer to a large greased glass or ceramic baking dish and bake for 1 hour, until lightly browned and bubbly.

3. Remove from the oven and let cool for about half an hour before serving. If the pudding has developed a skin on top, skim it off before serving. Garnish with the ice cream and mint leaves, or layer with tofu whip for a parfait, if desired.

JORGE'S OATMEAL CURRANT COOKIES

makes 18 cookies

These cookies, which were developed by our very talented pastry chef Jorge Pineda, are fun and easy to make. They're great to pack into lunch boxes for kids of all ages.

---

1 ½ CUPS ROLLED OATS

¾ CUP UNBLEACHED WHITE FLOUR

½ TEASPOON BAKING SODA

¼ TEASPOON GROUND CINNAMON

½ TEASPOON SEA SALT (FINE-GRAINED)

2 TABLESPOONS EGG REPLACER

1 CUP RAISINS OR CURRANTS

1 CUP UNREFINED SUGAR

½ CUP SPECTRUM SPREAD

1 TEASPOON VANILLA EXTRACT

1. Preheat the oven to 325°F. Line baking sheets with parchment paper.

2. In a large bowl, combine the rolled oats, unbleached flour, baking soda, cinnamon, and salt and mix together well. In another large bowl, whisk the egg replacer until foamy. Add the raisins, sugar, Spectrum Spread, and vanilla to the egg replacer and mix well to combine. Stir the wet mixture into the flour mixture and mix well to combine.

3. Spoon 2 tablespoons of the dough for each cookie and place onto the baking sheets. Wet your hands with water and press the dough down into round cookies. Bake for 10 to 15 minutes, or until the cookies are lightly browned.

OATMEAL CHOCOLATE CHIP COOKIES

makes about 18 cookies

We sell these healthy cookies at the juice bar in the cafe.
They fly out of the restaurant as fast as we make them.

---

1 CUP ROLLED OATS

1 CUP SPELT FLOUR

¼ CUP BROWN RICE FLOUR

¼ TEASPOON BAKING POWDER

¼ TEASPOON SEA SALT (FINE-GRAINED)

½ CUP SAFFLOWER OIL

1 CUP MAPLE SYRUP

¼ TEASPOON VANILLA EXTRACT

¼ TEASPOON ALMOND EXTRACT

1 TABLESPOON EGG REPLACER

1 CUP DAIRY-FREE CHOCOLATE CHIPS (SEE NOTE)

1. Preheat the oven to 350°F.

2. In a large mixing bowl, combine the oats, flours, baking soda, and salt. Add the oil, ¼ cup of water, the maple syrup, vanilla and almond extracts, and egg replacer and stir well to combine. Fold the chocolate chips into the batter.

3. Spoon tablespoons of batter onto a large baking sheet and space them 3 inches apart. Flatten the batter with the back of a wet spoon. Bake for 10 to 15 minutes, until lightly browned. Remove the cookies from the baking sheet and let cool on wire racks.

NOTE: Dairy-free chocolate chips are available at health food stores or online.

MACAROONS

makes about 36 cookies

Coconut lovers really flip for this wheat-free version of the classic macaroon, made with carrots, almonds, and maple syrup.

---

1 ¼ CUPS SPELT FLOUR

1 ¾ CUPS UNSWEETENED SHREDDED COCONUT

2 TEASPOONS ARROWROOT

1 CUP GRATED CARROTS

½ CUP SLICED ALMONDS

¾ CUP MAPLE SYRUP

⅓ CUP SAFFLOWER OIL

2 TABLESPOONS EGG REPLACER

1 ½ TEASPOONS ALMOND EXTRACT

1 TEASPOON GRATED LEMON ZEST

1. Preheat the oven to 300°F.

2. In a large mixing bowl, mix together the flour, coconut, and arrowroot. In another bowl, mix together the carrots, almonds, ¼ cup of water, the maple syrup, oil, egg replacer, almond extract, and lemon zest. Add the wet mixture to the flour mixture and stir well to combine.

3. Spoon large balls of dough onto baking sheets (a small ice cream scoop is perfect for this). Bake for 30 minutes, until the coconut looks toasted. Remove the cookies from the baking sheets and let cool on wire racks.

BRITSY BRITTLES

makes about 36 cookies

These cookies are one of the first we ever made at Candle Cafe.
They're very crunchy, like peanut brittle, and can be crumbled over
pudding or mousse. While still warm, they can also be shaped into tuiles
and filled with ice cream for a scrumptious dessert.

1 CUP OAT FLOUR

¾ CUP ROLLED OATS

3 TABLESPOONS GROUND CINNAMON

1 TEASPOON BAKING POWDER

1 TEASPOON SEA SALT (FINE-GRAINED)

2 TABLESPOONS SAFFLOWER OIL

1¼ CUPS BROWN RICE SYRUP

¼ CUP MAPLE SYRUP

½ CUP WALNUTS

½ CUP RAISINS

½ CUP PITTED AND FINELY CHOPPED
   DATES

1. Preheat the oven to 350°F. Line baking sheets with parchment paper.

2. In a large mixing bowl, combine the flour, oats, cinnamon, baking powder, and salt. In
   another bowl, whisk together the oil, brown rice syrup, and maple syrup. Add the wet
   ingredients to the flour mixture and stir well to combine. Fold in the walnuts, raisins, and
   dates and mix well. Set aside for about 20 minutes.

3. Spoon about 2 tablespoons of batter for each cookie, spaced an inch apart, onto the
   baking sheets. Bake for 11 to 12 minutes, until lightly browned. Remove and let cool for
   about 10 minutes before transferring to wire racks.

CHOCOLATE MACADAMIA NUT COOKIES

makes about 18 cookies

These rich and delicious cookies are just the thing for a
late afternoon or evening snack.

---

1 CUP UNBLEACHED ALL-PURPOSE
FLOUR

1 CUP UNREFINED SUGAR

1 CUP DAIRY-FREE CHOCOLATE CHIPS

¾ CUP UNSWEETENED COCOA POWDER

½ TEASPOON BAKING SODA

⅛ TEASPOON SEA SALT (FINE-GRAINED)

1 CUP CHOPPED MACADAMIA NUTS

½ CUP SOY MARGARINE

1 TABLESPOON EGG REPLACER

1 TEASPOON VANILLA EXTRACT

1. Preheat the oven to 350°F. Grease baking sheets or line them with baking parchment.

2. In a large mixing bowl, mix together the flour, sugar, chocolate chips, cocoa powder,
baking soda, salt, and nuts. In another bowl, whisk together the margarine, egg replacer,
and vanilla. Pour the wet ingredients into the dry mixture and mix well to combine.

3. Using a tablespoon, drop the batter 2 inches apart onto the baking sheets. Bake for 15 to
20 minutes, until the bottoms of the cookies begin to brown.

DATE CRUMB SQUARES

makes 12 squares

Date Crumb Squares have long been a Candle favorite. They're a great healthy snack and a good treat to pack in a lunch box. Start soaking the dates a day before you want to bake the squares.

½ CUP WHOLE PITTED DATES

4 CUPS OAT FLOUR

4 CUPS ROLLED OATS

¾ CUP CHOPPED WALNUTS OR PECANS

1 CUP SAFFLOWER OIL

1 CUP MAPLE SYRUP

1 TEASPOON ALMOND EXTRACT

½ TEASPOON SEA SALT (FINE-GRAINED)

1. The day before, soak the dates in 1 cup of water to soften. Drain, put the dates in a food processor, and process until smooth.

2. Preheat the oven to 350°F.

3. In a large bowl, combine the flour, rolled oats, and walnuts or pecans and mix together well. In another bowl, blend together the safflower oil, maple syrup, almond extract, and sea salt. Add the wet ingredients to the flour mixture and mix well. Press half of the mixture into a greased 12 X 6-inch baking pan. Spread the puréed dates over the mixture, top with the remaining half of the flour mixture, and press down lightly. Bake for 30 minutes, or until lightly browned. Let cool and cut into squares.

CHOCOLATE BROWNIES

makes 12 to 16 brownies

These brownies are made with the most surprising ingredient—beets! They are a natural sweetener and bring out the dark richness of the chocolate.

———◆———

1 MEDIUM BEET, TRIMMED	½ CUP WHOLE WHEAT PASTRY FLOUR
½ CUP DAIRY-FREE CHOCOLATE CHIPS	1½ CUPS UNBLEACHED FLOUR
⅓ CUP MAPLE SYRUP	½ TEASPOON BAKING POWDER
1 CUP UNREFINED SUGAR	½ TEASPOON BAKING SODA
½ CUP CHOPPED DATES	1 CUP UNSWEETENED COCOA POWDER
8 OUNCES SILKEN TOFU	¼ TEASPOON SEA SALT (FINE-GRAINED)
½ TABLESPOON VANILLA EXTRACT	¼ CUP BARLEY MALT (SEE NOTE)
1 CUP SPECTRUM SPREAD OR OTHER SOY MARGARINE	¼ CUP CHOPPED PECANS

1. To prepare the beet, preheat the oven to 350°F. Wrap the beet in tinfoil, place in a small baking pan, and bake until tender, about 1 hour. When cool enough to handle, peel, chop coarsely, and set aside.

2. Reduce the heat to 325°F. Lightly grease a 9 × 13-inch baking pan or line the pan with baking parchment.

3. In the top of a double boiler over simmering water, combine ¼ cup of the chocolate chips and the maple syrup. Stir frequently until the chocolate is almost melted. Remove from the heat and stir to melt completely.

4. In a blender, combine the sugar with the chocolate mixture. Add the beet, dates, silken tofu, vanilla, and Spectrum Spread and continue to blend until very smooth.

5. Sift the flours into a large mixing bowl. Add the baking powder, baking soda, cocoa powder, and salt and stir well. Add the chocolate mixture and the barley malt to the flour mixture and stir well to combine.

6. Pour the mixture into the baking pan. Bake for 30 to 35 minutes, or until a cake tester or toothpick inserted into the center comes out clean. Remove from the oven and top with the pecans and the remaining chocolate chips. Transfer to wire racks and let cool completely. Slice the brownies to your taste and serve.

NOTE: Barley malt is a mild liquid sweetener with a molasses-like consistency. It is available in health food stores.

CHOCOLATE-DIPPED STRAWBERRIES

makes 24

Chocolate-covered strawberries, a well-known aphrodisiac, are always a hit at the restaurant. They are always on our special Valentine's Day menu as a romantic end to the meal. You can also dip dried apricots and pears in chocolate for a delicious treat.

1 CUP (8 OUNCES) SWEET DARK DAIRY-FREE CHOCOLATE CHIPS OR PIECES (SEE NOTE)

2 POUNDS FRESH, LONG-STEMMED STRAWBERRIES

1. Line a baking sheet with baking parchment or wax paper.

2. In the top of a double boiler over boiling water, melt the chocolate, stirring occasionally. When melted, turn the heat down to a gentle simmer. Dip the strawberries halfway into the melted chocolate, then carefully transfer them to the baking sheet, spacing them an inch apart from each other. Let cool a bit before serving.

NOTE: There are many good brands of organic chocolate. We like Green and Black's, Rapunzel, Dagoba, and Tropical Source.

VANILLA-SCENTED POACHED PEARS

serves 4

Our recipe tester, Stephanie, inspired by the late-summer fruit she saw at the farmer's market, created this fantastic recipe using fresh ripe pears.

---

4 MEDIUM PEARS, WASHED AND
  PEELED

¼ CUP FRESH LEMON JUICE

¼ CUP CRANBERRIES

½ CUP SLICED TOASTED ALMONDS
  (SEE PAGE 181)

1 TEASPOON GROUND CINNAMON

2 CINNAMON STICKS

½ CUP APPLE JUICE

2 TEASPOONS VANILLA EXTRACT

1. Peel the pears and cut them in half from stem to base. Core the pears and leave the bottoms intact. Drizzle them with the lemon juice.

2. Fill each pear with an equal portion of cranberries and almonds. Sprinkle the pears lightly with the cinnamon. Arrange the pears, filled side up, in a saucepan. Add the cinnamon sticks to the pan and pour the apple juice and vanilla extract around the pears. Simmer, uncovered, over medium heat for 20 to 25 minutes, or until tender.

BREAD AND BREAKFAST

Freshly baked Cinnamon Crumb Coffee Cake and Lemon—Poppy Seed Muffins; homemade pancakes and French toast; granola and porridge made from scratch —such is the fare you might imagine in the breakfast counter of your dreams.

This chapter has a delightful array of breakfast treats for you to make. These healthy and delicious recipes are easy to prepare and so soul-warming, whether you're eating breakfast on the run or making a meal for a leisurely Sunday morning. So dream no more.

MAUI MUFFINS
WITH ORANGE GLAZE

makes 12 muffins

These muffins, loaded with tropical flavors, are a great way to start the day.
They are simply delicious and will fuel you all morning.

1 CUP ALL-PURPOSE FLOUR

1 CUP WHOLE WHEAT PASTRY FLOUR

2 TEASPOONS BAKING POWDER

½ TEASPOON BAKING SODA

¼ TEASPOON SEA SALT (FINE-GRAINED)

1½ TEASPOONS EGG REPLACER

¾ CUP ORANGE JUICE

¼ CUP AGAVE NECTAR

1½ TABLESPOONS GRATED ORANGE ZEST

¼ CUP SAFFLOWER OIL

½ CUP UNSWEETENED SHREDDED
COCONUT

½ CUP DICED PINEAPPLE

ORANGE GLAZE

1 CUP CONFECTIONERS' SUGAR
(SEE NOTE)

4 TABLESPOONS ORANGE JUICE

2 TEASPOONS GRATED ORANGE ZEST

1. Preheat the oven to 350°F.

2. In a large bowl, combine the flours, baking powder, baking soda, and salt and whisk. In a separate bowl, dissolve the egg replacer into the orange juice, then add 1 cup of water, the agave nectar, orange zest, and safflower oil and mix until smooth. Combine the wet ingredients with the flour mixture. Fold in the coconut and pineapple.

3. Grease a muffin tin with soy margarine or use cupcake papers to line the tin. Pour the batter into the muffin tin almost to the top and bake for 20 to 25 minutes, or until a cake tester or toothpick comes out clean. Set aside to cool.

4. To make the orange glaze, heat the orange juice in a small pot until bubbly, then add confectioners' sugar and zest. Take off heat and let stand until muffins are ready, then drizzle glaze on top of muffins and serve at once.

NOTE: Edward & Sons brand of organic confectioners' sugar is available in health food stores.

VARIATION: This recipe can also be made into a sheet cake, as we did for our great friend Kitty's birthday. Use a 13 x 9-inch pan, and increase baking time to 30 minutes.

LEMON–POPPY SEED MUFFINS

makes 12 muffins

Who doesn't love light, citrusy Lemon–Poppy Seed Muffins? Plenty of customers at the Candle enjoy these with their morning soy lattes.

––––––––◆––––––––

1 CUP WHOLE WHEAT FLOUR

1 CUP UNBLEACHED FLOUR

¼ CUP UNREFINED SUGAR

1 TEASPOON BAKING SODA

2 TEASPOONS BAKING POWDER

½ TEASPOON SEA SALT (FINE-GRAINED)

½ CUP SOY MARGARINE, PREFERABLY SOY GARDEN BRAND

½ CUP MAPLE SYRUP

½ CUP SOY MILK

¼ CUP LEMON JUICE

¼ CUP POPPY SEEDS

2 TEASPOONS GRATED LEMON ZEST

1. Preheat the oven to 350°F. Grease a muffin tin or line tins with cupcake papers.

2. Sift the flours, sugar, baking soda, baking powder, and salt into a large mixing bowl and whisk to mix. In a separate bowl, whisk together the margarine, maple syrup, soy milk, and lemon juice until foamy. Pour the wet ingredients into the flour mixture and mix until the batter is smooth. Fold in the poppy seeds and lemon zest.

3. Pour the batter into the muffin tins, dividing evenly. Bake on a center rack of the oven for 20 to 25 minutes, or until a cake tester or toothpick inserted into the center comes out clean. Serve at once.

CINNAMON CRUMB COFFEE CAKE

serves 6 to 8

Our house mom, Theresa, makes sure we all have a delicious breakfast every morning so we're good and ready to serve our wonderful customers! Thanks, Theresa!

CAKE

1 CUP SPECTRUM SPREAD OR OTHER SOY MARGARINE

1½ CUPS UNREFINED SUGAR

1 TABLESPOON EGG REPLACER DISSOLVED IN ¼ CUP HOT WATER

1½ TEASPOONS VANILLA EXTRACT

1 CUP WHOLE WHEAT PASTRY FLOUR

1 CUP UNBLEACHED ALL-PURPOSE FLOUR

1 TEASPOON BAKING POWDER

1 TEASPOON BAKING SODA

½ TEASPOON SEA SALT (FINE-GRAINED)

SOY SOUR CREAM

½ POUND FIRM TOFU, RINSED AND WELL DRAINED

¼ CUP SAFFLOWER OIL

DASH OF FRESH LEMON JUICE

1 TABLESPOON APPLE CIDER VINEGAR

1½ TEASPOONS SEA SALT (FINE-GRAINED)

TOPPING

1 CUP UNREFINED SUGAR

2 TEASPOONS GROUND CINNAMON

⅓ CUP ROUGHLY CHOPPED PECANS

⅓ CUP ROUGHLY CHOPPED ALMONDS

½ CUP SPECTRUM SPREAD OR OTHER SOY MARGARINE

1. Preheat the oven to 350°F.

2. To make the cake, cream the soy margarine, sugar, and dissolved egg replacer in a large bowl with an electric mixer or fork. Stir in the vanilla. Sift together the flours, baking powder, baking soda, and salt and set aside.

3. To make the soy sour cream, place the tofu, safflower oil, lemon juice, vinegar, and salt in a blender and blend until smooth.

4. Combine the flour mixture with the wet mixture and fold in the sour cream. Mix together until well combined.

5. To make the topping, mix together the sugar, cinnamon, pecans, almonds, and soy margarine until well coated with the margarine.

6. Pour half the batter into an oiled 9-inch pie pan. Sprinkle with half the topping, add the remaining batter, and sprinkle with the remaining topping. Bake for about 30 to 40 minutes. Remove from the oven and let cool in the pan. Cut into wedges and serve.

DINER-STYLE PANCAKES

serves 4 to 6

Whether you eat these delicious vegan pancakes for breakfast, brunch,
or a midnight snack, you'll love 'em.

———◆———

1¼ CUPS SIFTED UNBLEACHED WHITE
   OR SPELT FLOUR

2½ TEASPOONS BAKING POWDER

 2 TABLESPOONS UNREFINED SUGAR

¾ TEASPOON SEA SALT (FINE-GRAINED)

1½ TEASPOONS EGG REPLACER
   DISSOLVED IN 1 TABLESPOON SOY
   MILK

1¾ CUPS SOY MILK

½ TEASPOON VANILLA EXTRACT

 3 TABLESPOONS SAFFLOWER OIL, PLUS
   OIL FOR COOKING THE PANCAKES

SOY MARGARINE (OPTIONAL)

MAPLE SYRUP (OPTIONAL)

1. In a large mixing bowl, combine the flour, baking powder, sugar, and salt. In a separate
   bowl, combine the dissolved egg replacer, soy milk, vanilla extract, and oil. Mix the flour
   mixture and the egg mixture together, stirring well to combine.

2. In a large skillet over medium-high heat, heat some oil. Drop large spoonfuls of batter onto
   the skillet, leaving room for the pancakes to expand. Cook until the bottoms are golden
   and bubbles are popping on the surface, about 2 to 3 minutes. Flip the pancakes and cook
   until golden. Repeat, using up all the batter. Serve with soy margarine and maple syrup,
   if desired.

WHEAT-FREE PANCAKES

serves 4 to 6

This is a great alternative for breakfast for those staying away from wheat.
We like to add sliced bananas, fresh blueberries, or vegan chocolate chips
to the pancakes for an additional taste treat.

FLAX EGGS

²⁄₃ CUP WARM WATER

¹⁄₃ CUP FLAX SEEDS

PANCAKES

³⁄₄ CUP CORNMEAL

¹⁄₄ CUP BLUE CORNMEAL

³⁄₄ CUP SPELT FLOUR

³⁄₄ CUP OAT FLOUR

¹⁄₄ CUP BROWN RICE FLOUR

1 TABLESPOON BAKING POWDER

¹⁄₂ TEASPOON BAKING SODA

¹⁄₂ TEASPOON SEA SALT (FINE-GRAINED)

2 CUPS SOY MILK

1 TABLESPOON AGAVE NECTAR

1 TABLESPOON SAFFLOWER OIL, PLUS
  OIL FOR COOKING THE PANCAKES

1. To make the flax eggs, place the warm water in a blender container and add the flax seeds. Let sit for 15 minutes, then blend at high speed until gelatinous and the flax seeds are no longer visible. (The remaining flax eggs will keep, covered, in the refrigerator for up to 2 weeks.)

2. In a large mixing bowl, combine the cornmeals, flours, baking powder, baking soda, and salt. In a separate bowl, combine 1 tablespoon of flax eggs (see Note), the soy milk, agave nectar, and oil. Mix the flour mixture together with the soy milk mixture, stirring well to combine.

3. In a large skillet over medium high-heat, heat some oil. Drop large spoonfuls of the batter onto the skillet, leaving room for the pancakes to expand. Cook until the bottoms are golden and bubbles are popping on the surface, 2 to 3 minutes. Flip the pancakes and cook until golden. Repeat, using up all the batter.

NOTE: A tablespoon of flax eggs is equivalent to 1 egg.

VANILLA-CINNAMON FRENCH TOAST

serves 4 to 6

This yummy French toast is an early-morning treat, especially when topped with fresh berries and a sprinkle of confectioners' sugar. For wheat-free French toast, substitute spelt bread for the sourdough.

1 POUND SILKEN TOFU

1 ¼ CUPS VANILLA RICE MILK

4 ½ TEASPOONS AGAVE NECTAR

3 ¾ TEASPOONS GROUND CINNAMON

1 TEASPOON VANILLA EXTRACT

6 TO 8 SLICES OF SOURDOUGH OR SPELT BREAD

COCONUT BUTTER OR SAFFLOWER OIL, FOR COOKING THE FRENCH TOAST

FRESH STRAWBERRIES, BLUEBERRIES, OR BLACKBERRIES (OPTIONAL)

CONFECTIONERS' SUGAR (OPTIONAL)

1. In a blender container, combine the tofu, rice milk, agave nectar, cinnamon, and vanilla and blend on high speed until smooth. The consistency should be fairly liquid, so add additional rice milk if necessary. Pour the mixture into a shallow bowl. Add the bread slices and immerse both sides of the bread in the batter until soaked through.

2. In a large skillet over medium heat, heat some butter or oil. Cook each side for 4 to 6 minutes, or until the bread begins to brown lightly. The toast should feel slightly crispy before removing from the skillet. Serve with fresh berries and confectioners' sugar, if desired.

TOFU SCRAMBLE WITH YUKON GOLD AND SWEET POTATO HOME FRIES

serves 4 to 6

We like to whip up this delicious tofu scramble with home fries made from Yukon Gold and sweet potatoes on lazy weekend mornings. Begin to cook the scramble just as the home fries are nearly browned to perfection so you can serve this hearty and soul-satisfying breakfast all at once. It tastes and looks great when accompanied by salsa or chopped tomatoes and a handful of garden-fresh herbs.

1 TABLESPOON EXTRA-VIRGIN OLIVE OIL

1 ONION, DICED

1 GREEN BELL PEPPER, SEEDED, DEVEINED, AND DICED

½ RED BELL PEPPER, SEEDED, DEVEINED, AND DICED

1 TABLESPOON GROUND CUMIN

1 TABLESPOON GROUND TURMERIC

1 TEASPOON CORIANDER

½ TEASPOON CHILI POWDER

½ TEASPOON PAPRIKA

1 TEASPOON DRIED THYME
PINCH OF CAYENNE

¼ TEASPOON SEA SALT
FRESHLY GROUND BLACK PEPPER

2 POUNDS FIRM TOFU, DRAINED OF EXCESS WATER
YUKON GOLD AND SWEET POTATO HOME FRIES (RECIPE FOLLOWS)

1. In a sauté pan, heat the olive oil and add the onion and peppers. Cook until softened, about 5 minutes.

2. In a small bowl, mix together the cumin, turmeric, coriander, chili powder, paprika, thyme, cayenne, salt, and pepper, and set aside.

3. Crumble the tofu into bite-sized pieces with a fork and add to the sauté pan. Sprinkle the spice mixture over the tofu to coat and sauté for about 5 minutes. Serve at once with the home fries.

YUKON GOLD AND SWEET POTATO HOME FRIES

serves 4 to 6

2 TABLESPOONS EXTRA-VIRGIN OLIVE OIL

1 ONION, CHOPPED

1 RED BELL PEPPER, SEEDED, DEVEINED, AND DICED

1 JALAPEÑO PEPPER, SEEDED AND DICED

4 TO 5 YUKON GOLD POTATOES, PEELED AND CUT INTO 1-INCH DICE

1 SWEET POTATO, PEELED AND CUT INTO 1-INCH DICE

1 TEASPOON DRIED OREGANO

1 TEASPOON DRIED THYME

1 TEASPOON SEA SALT

FRESHLY GROUND BLACK PEPPER

In a sauté pan over medium heat, heat 1 tablespoon of the oil. Add the onion and peppers and cook until the onion is softened, about 5 minutes. Add the remaining oil, then add the potatoes, oregano, thyme, salt, and pepper to taste. Lower the heat and continue to cook, stirring often, until the potatoes are nicely browned, 20 to 25 minutes. Serve at once.

BREAKFAST BURRITO WITH RANCHEROS SAUCE

makes 1 large burrito, serves 2

Here's a terrific way to start the day—with a tasty tortilla filled with steamed spinach, black beans, rice, and Tofu Scramble. Topped with spicy rancheros sauce, it makes a delicious Southwestern-style breakfast.

RANCHEROS SAUCE

- 1 TABLESPOON EXTRA-VIRGIN OLIVE OIL
- 3 GARLIC CLOVES, PEELED
- 1 DRIED PASILLA PEPPER
- 1 CUP COARSELY CHOPPED FRESH OR CANNED, PREFERABLY ORGANIC, TOMATOES
- 2 LARGE ONIONS, COARSELY CHOPPED
- 1 TEASPOON CHOPPED GARLIC
- 1 TEASPOON DRIED THYME
- 1 TEASPOON DRIED OREGANO
- ¼ TEASPOON CAYENNE (OPTIONAL)

BURRITO

- ¼ CUP FRESH SPINACH, STEAMED AND DRAINED
- ½ CUP COOKED BLACK BEANS
- ¼ CUP COOKED BROWN RICE
- ½ CUP TOFU SCRAMBLE (PAGE 204)
- 1 10-INCH WHOLE WHEAT TORTILLA

1. To make the rancheros sauce, preheat the oven to 300°F. In a small baking dish, put the olive oil and garlic and bake for 15 to 20 minutes. Add the pasilla pepper and bake for an additional 5 minutes. Remove from the oven and let cool.

2. Transfer the roasted garlic and pepper to a blender. Add the tomatoes, onions, garlic, thyme, oregano, and cayenne, if using, and blend until smooth.

3. To assemble the burrito, place the spinach, beans, rice, and Tofu Scramble over the tortilla and roll one of the long sides. Fold the sides of each end, then roll up the other side. Cut the burrito in half. Heat the rancheros sauce until warmed through, drizzle over the burrito, and serve at once.

CANDLE CAFE GRANOLA

makes 4 cups, serves 8

Our house-favorite granola is great in many ways—serve it with soy or rice milk, stir into yogurt, or just eat by the handful as a snack. We also like to add dried blueberries and cranberries—even chocolate chips—to this delicious pantry staple. The possibilities are endless.

1 CUP STEEL-CUT OATS

½ CUP ROLLED OATS

¼ CUP SLIVERED ALMONDS

¾ CUP COARSELY CHOPPED WALNUTS

¼ CUP RAW SUNFLOWER SEEDS

⅓ CUP MAPLE SYRUP

¼ CUP SAFFLOWER OR COCONUT OIL

1 TABLESPOON VANILLA EXTRACT

¼ TEASPOON SEA SALT

½ CUP RAISINS

¼ CUP UNSWEETENED SHREDDED COCONUT

1. Preheat the oven to 350°F. Line a baking sheet with baking parchment.

2. Combine the steel-cut and rolled oats, the almonds, walnuts, sunflower seeds, maple syrup, oil, vanilla, and salt. Spread out on the baking sheet and bake for 20 minutes, until golden, stirring every 5 minutes. Remove from the oven and let cool. Transfer to a bowl and stir in the raisins and shredded coconut. The granola will keep, in an air-tight container, for up to one month.

POWER PORRIDGE WITH COCONUT-PECAN MARMALADE

serves 4 to 6

Start your morning with this fabulous porridge, scented with cloves and cardamom,
and topped with toasty coconut-pecan marmalade.

3 CUPS SOY MILK

1 ½ CUPS STEEL-CUT OATS

½ CUP QUINOA, RINSED SEVERAL TIMES

¼ CUP UNREFINED SUGAR

¼ TEASPOON GROUND CLOVES

¼ TEASPOON CARDAMOM

PINCH OF SEA SALT

COCONUT-PECAN MARMALADE

½ CUP CHOPPED AND TOASTED PECANS (SEE NOTE)

½ CUP TOASTED UNSWEETENED COCONUT (SEE NOTE)

1 CUP COCONUT MILK

⅓ CUP AGAVE NECTAR

¾ TEASPOON VANILLA EXTRACT

¾ TEASPOON COCONUT EXTRACT

1. In a large saucepan, bring the soy milk and 3 cups of water to a boil over medium-high heat. Add the oats, quinoa, sugar, cloves, cardamom, and salt and cook, stirring occasionally, for 15 to 20 minutes, until creamy. Cover and let stand for 10 minutes.

2. To make the marmalade, stir the pecans, toasted coconut, coconut milk, agave nectar, and vanilla and coconut extracts together in a bowl until well blended.

3. Spoon the porridge into bowls and top with the marmalade. Serve with warmed almond milk or soy milk, if desired.

NOTE: To toast the pecans, spread them on a baking sheet and toast them in a preheated 350°F oven or toaster oven for about 5 minutes, or until golden brown. Shake the pan once or twice midway for even toasting. Slide the nuts off the baking sheet to stop the cooking.

To toast coconut, preheat the oven to 350°F. Spread the coconut on a baking sheet and bake until lightly browned, about 3 minutes.

GRILLED GINGER GRAPEFRUIT

serves 2

Here's a new and wonderful way to eat grapefruit—top it with sugar and ginger and broil it. The tangy grapefruit pairs very nicely with the sweet, spicy ginger.

———

1 WHOLE GRAPEFRUIT

1 TABLESPOON UNREFINED SUGAR

1 TEASPOON PEELED AND MINCED FRESH GINGER

Cut the grapefruit in half. In a small dish, mix together the sugar and ginger and sprinkle over the grapefruit. Place on a baking sheet and put it under an oven broiler or in a toaster oven. Broil for 6 minutes, until the sugar and ginger start to bubble and caramelize.

BEAN, LEGUME, AND GRAIN COOKING GUIDES

Grains and beans vary in cooking and soaking times. These charts are an easy way to make sure they'll be cooked properly.

GRAIN COOKING CHART

GRAIN (1 CUP DRY)	CUPS WATER	COOK TIME	CUPS YIELD
Amaranth	2½	20–25 min.	2½
Barley, flakes	3	20 min.	2½
Barley, hulled	3	1¼ hrs.	3½
Barley, pearled	3	50–60 min.	3½
Buckwheat groats*	2	15 min.	2½
Cornmeal (fine grind)	4–4½	8–10 min.	2½
Cornmeal (polenta, coarse)	4–4½	20–25 min.	2½
Cornmeal grits	4	15–20 min.	4
Millet, hulled	3–4	20–25 min.	3½
Oat bran	2½	5 min.	2
Oat groats	3	30–40 min.	3½
Quinoa†	2	15–20 min.	2¾
Rice, brown basmati	2½	35–40 min.	3
Rice, brown, long grain	2½	45–55 min.	3
Rice, brown, quick	1¼	10 min.	2
Rice, brown, short grain‡	2–2½	45–55 min.	3
Rice, wild	3	50–60 min.	4
Rye berries	3–4	1 hr.	3
Rye flakes	2	10–15 min.	3
Spelt	3–4	40–50 min.	2½
Wheat, bulgur	2	15 min.	2½
Wheat, couscous	1	5 min.	2
Wheat, cracked	2	20–25 min.	2¼
Wheat, whole berries	3	2 hrs.	2½

*Buckwheat groats are available toasted and untoasted. Cooking times are the same.

†Quinoa should be well rinsed in a fine strainer for 2 to 3 minutes to remove the saponens (a natural, protective coating that will give a bitter flavor if not rinsed off).

‡Short-grain brown rice is sometimes labeled sweet, glutinous, or sticky brown rice.

TIPS FOR COOKING BEANS
AND LEGUMES

To prepare beans or legumes, sort, wash, and drain them. To increase the digestibility of beans, soak them in water, preferably for 8 hours or overnight, with a 3-inch piece of kombu seaweed.

If you don't have enough time for an overnight soak, bring the beans to a boil for 3 minutes and let sit for 2 hours off the heat. Discard the soaking water and cover the beans and kombu with fresh water.

To cook the beans or legumes, put them in a large pot and cover with ample water. Bring to a boil and skim off the foam, then cover and reduce the heat, simmering until tender. Beans and legumes double in volume when cooked, so if a recipe calls for 2 cups of cooked beans, you'll need to start out with 1 cup of raw beans. Specific cooking times are listed below.

BEAN AND LEGUME COOKING CHART

BEAN	MINIMUM SOAK TIME	BOIL TIME (VARIES ACCORDING TO SOAK TIME. COOK UNTIL TENDER.)
Small: Adzuki, lentil, split pea	1–2 hours (optional)	30 minutes–1 hour
Medium: Navy, black-eyed pea, black bean	4–6 hours	1½ hours
Large: Pinto bean, chickpea, kidney bean, white bean	6–8 hours	1½–2 hours

GLOSSARY

ADZUKI BEANS

Small, shiny dark red beans from Japan that provide high-quality protein. Easily digested, they are considered a healing food.

AGAR-AGAR

(Also called agar powder) A seaweed product used as a gelling agent. Rich in calcium; no calories and soothing to the digestive tract.

AGAVE NECTAR

Natural sweetener derived from a succulent, cactuslike plant, with the color and consistency of honey. A very versatile syrup used in many desserts.

AMARANTH

A tiny, seedlike grain, usually yellow-brown in color. Rich in protein and aminos and often used in healthy cereals.

ARAME

A sea vegetable that's very high in calcium, potassium, iron, protein, and vitamins A, B_1, and B_2. Use in salads and with vegetables and tofu.

ARROWROOT POWDER

A thickening agent made from arrowroot, a tropical tuber. It is more easily digested than wheat and is high in calcium. Use in puddings, sauces, and other foods.

BROWN RICE SYRUP

A natural sweetener made from fermented rice grain, similar to barley malt. It can be used in place of maple syrup. Very good for the body's mineral balance.

BROWN RICE VINEGAR

An organic, naturally brown, unfiltered and unpasteurized vinegar made from brown rice wine.

CHIPOTLE PEPPER, DRIED OR POWDERED

Smoked, hot, and spicy jalapeño peppers. Use to give a smoky, savory flavor to chilis, soups, and sandwich spreads.

COCONUT BUTTER

A coconut-based oil substitute with a mild, light, and creamy flavor. Use for baking and sautéed dishes. Excellent in piecrusts.

DULSE

A sea vegetable with the highest concentration of iron of any food source. Use in vegetables, soups, and salads.

FLAX SEED OIL

An omega-3 oil, this oil is easily digestible and very nutritious. Use in salad dressings and sauces. Also good drizzled over cereal and porridge and as a spread for bread.

HERBAMARE

A powdered condiment with an array of garlic, herbs, and sea salt used to enhance flavors.

HIZIKI

A sea vegetable that's very high in calcium, phosphorus, iron, protein, and vitamins A, B_1, and B_2. Use in soups, salads, and as a garnish.

KOMBU

A flat, wide sea vegetable that's very high in calcium, phosphorus, iron, protein, vitamins A, B_1, B_2, and C. Chop and add to salads and vegetables. Add unsoaked to soups for a rich stock. When soaked and cooked with beans, kombu increases their digestibility.

KUZU

A natural thickening agent derived from the root of the kuzu vine. Has a slight medicinal flavor and is soothing to the intestines. Use in sauces and to coat foods before frying for a crisp crust.

LAVASH

A nonfat whole wheat Middle Eastern flatbread.

MILLET

A small, quick-cooking yellow grain with a nutty flavor. It is gluten-free, easily digestible, and high in protein and nutrients.

MISO

Fermented soybean paste whose flavor is affected by its aging process, which can range from six months to three years. There are three categories of miso: barley miso, which is dark in color; soybean miso, which is medium in color; and rice miso, which is lighter. This mainstay of Japanese cooking is rich in amino acids and live enzymes. It is an excellent source of protein and a remarkable digestive aid. Use the lighter miso in delicate soups, broths, and sauces and the darker-colored miso in heavier stewed dishes.

NORI

A sea vegetable that's very high in calcium, phosphorus, iron, protein, potassium, magnesium, iodine, vitamins A, B_1, B_2, C, D, and niacin. Use sprinkled over vegetables, grains, and salads, or rolled around rice and vegetable fillings.

NUTRITIONAL YEAST FLAKES

Dried flakes derived from yeast that are high in vitamins and minerals. Use in small amounts to add body and flavor to soups, stocks, and salad dressings.

ORGANIC

Term applied to foods with no synthetic chemicals, herbicides, pesticides, chemical fertilizers, or fungicides.

QUINOA

First cultivated by the Incas, this unique grain has complete protein and is packed with lysine and other amino acids. Rich source of calcium, iron, phosphorus, various B vitamins, and vitamin E.

SEA SALT

Derived from evaporated sea water, this flavorful salt is high in trace minerals. It comes in fine-grained and larger crystals.

SEITAN

Often called wheat meat, this chewy wheat gluten is naturally high in protein, low in carbohydrates and fat. It is often served as a main dish in vegan cooking and is an excellent meat substitute.

SESAME TAHINI

Hulled sesame seeds ground into a paste; rich in calcium, phosphorus, and protein. A staple of the Middle Eastern diet, it is used in Hummus and babaganoush.

SHOYU AND TAMARI SOY SAUCE

Traditional Japanese soy sauce made from fermented whole soybeans. Nama Shoyu is an unpasteurized variety. Tamari is available in a wheat-free version. All varieties are interchangeable in recipes.

SOY CHEESE

Vegan cheese made from soybeans, similar in texture to dairy cheese such as mozzarella. Use in pasta dishes, quesadillas, pizzas, and sandwiches.

SOY MARGARINE

Made from soybeans, this dairy-free margarine has a buttery texture. Use in baking.

SOY MILK

Milk made from soybeans pressed in water, then filtered and rehydrated. Good source of vegetable protein. Packaged organic brands are readily available.

SUCANAT

Organic dehydrated cane juice used as a natural sweetener.

TEMPEH

Traditional Indonesian fermented soy product that's heartier than tofu. High in protein, tempeh is chewy with a nutty flavor, and is easily digestible.

TEMPEH BACON

Tempeh that has been flattened into strips and flavored. Good in sandwiches and with breakfast and brunch dishes.

TOFU

Soy milk curds that are a good source of high-quality protein. Rich in calcium and cholesterol-free.

UMEBOSHI PASTE

Salty-sour pickled plum paste from Japan. It is puréed after aging with red shiso leaves. Good with tofu and vegetables.

UMEBOSHI VINEGAR

The brine from pickled umeboshi plums. Technically not a vinegar because it is not fermented, but it may be substituted for any vinegar.

UNREFINED SUGAR

A natural unrefined sweetener that comes from sugarcane. More nutritious than refined sugars.

WAKAME

A deep green, edible seaweed popular in Japan and other Asian countries. It's used like a vegetable in soups and simmered dishes, and occasionally in salads. It is rich in protein, calcium, iodine, magnesium, iron, and folate.

RESOURCE GUIDE

ALVARADO STREET BAKERY
500 Martin Ave.
Rohnert Park, CA 94928
707-585-3293
(fax) 707-585-8954
www.alvaradostreetbakery.com
Sprouted bagels, tortillas, breads

DAGOBA ORGANIC CHOCOLATE
P.O. Box 5330
Central Point, OR 97502-0053
541-664-9030
(fax) 541-664-9089
www.dagobachocolate.com
Organic chocolate products

EDEN FOODS, INC.
701 Tecumseh Rd.
Clinton, MI 49236
1-888-441-3336/517-456-7424
(fax) 517-456-7025
www.edenfoods.com
Specialty organic products

EDWARD & SONS
Box 1326
Carpinteria, CA 93014
805-684-8500
(fax) 805-684-8220
www.edwardandsons.com
Organic and vegan specialties

ENER-G FOODS INC.
5960 First Ave. South
Seattle, WA 98108
206-767-6660
(fax) 206-764-3398
www.ener-g.com
Gluten-free specialty foods and egg replacer

THE FILLO FACTORY, INC.
74 Cortland Ave.
Dumont, NJ 07628
201-439-1036
(fax) 201-385-0012
www.fillofactory.com
All types of phyllo products

FLORIDA CRYSTALS
One North Clematis St., Suite 200
West Palm Beach, FL 33401
800-558-8836/561-366-5148
(fax) 561-366-5158
www.floridacrystals.com
Organic natural sweeteners

**FOLLOW YOUR HEART
NATURAL FOODS**
P.O. Box 9400
Canoga Park, CA 91309-0400
818-348-3240
(fax) 818-348-1509
www.followyourheart.com
Vegan mayonnaise and cheeses

FOOD FOR LIFE BAKING CO.
2991 E. Doherty St.
Corona, CA 92879
909-279-5090
(fax) 909-279-1784
www.food-for-life.com
Wheat-free breads

FRENCH MEADOW
2610 Lyndale Ave. S.
Minneapolis, MN
612-870-4740
(fax) 612-870-0907
www.frenchmeadow.com
Specialty breads and flatbreads

FRESH TOFU, INC.
1101 Harrison St.
Allentown, PA 18103
610-433-4711
www.freshtofu.com
Certified organic tofu, tempeh, and seitan

FRONTIER NATURAL PRODUCTS
2990 Wilderness Place
Boulder, CO 80301
303-449-8137
(fax) 303-449-8139
www.frontiercoop.com
Herbs, spices, and organic flavor extracts

GFA BRANDS, INC.
P.O. Box 397
Cresskill, NJ 07626
201-568-9300
(fax) 201-568-6374
www.earthbalance.net
All-vegan buttery spreads

GOLDMINE NATURAL FOOD COMPANY
7805 Arjons Dr.
San Diego, CA 92126
800-475-FOOD
www.goldminenaturalfood.com
Organic and heirloom foods

JOSH'S ORGANIC GARDEN
Miami, Florida
954-456-FARM

LIGHT LIFE FOODS
153 Industrial Blvd.
Turners Falls, MA 01376
800-SOY-EASY
www.lightlife.com
Alternative meat sources

LUNDBERG FAMILY FARMS
P.O. Box 369
Richvale, CA 95974
www.lundberg.com
Specialty grains

MAINE COAST SEA VEGETABLES
3 George Pand Rd.
Franklin, ME 04634
207-565-2907
(fax) 207-565-2144
www.seaveg.com
Sea vegetables

MCFADDEN FARM
16000 Powerhouse Rd.
Potter Valley, CA 95469
800-544-8230
(fax) 707-743-1126
www.mcfaddenfarm.com
Certified organic herbs

MELISSA'S WORLD VARIETY PRODUCE, INC.
P.O. Box 21127
Los Angeles, CA
800-588-0151
www.melissas.com
Dried fruits and vegetables

MOUNTAIN DELL FARMS
2386 Roods Creek Rd.
Hancock, NY 13783
607-467-4034
Organic vegetables

OMEGA NUTRITION
800-661-3529
www.omegaflo.com
www.omeganutrition.com
Coconut butter and specialty oils

PURELY ORGANIC

P.O. Box 847
Fairfield, IA
641-472-7873
(fax) 641-472-1754
www.purelyorganic.com
*Organic gourmet Italian products, sun-dried
tomatoes you can eat straight from the package
(they require much less soaking time, too)*

RAPUNZEL PURE ORGANICS

2424 Route 203
Valatie, NY 12184
800-207-2814
www.rapunzel.com
Organic chocolate and sugar products

SHADY MAPLE FARM LTD.

2585 Skymark Ave., Suite 305
Mississauga, Ontario
L4W 4L5 Canada
905-206-1455
(fax) 905-206-1477
www.shadymaple.com
Organic maple syrup, sugar, and cookies

SOUTH RIVER MISO COMPANY, INC.

888 Shelburne Falls Rd.
Conway, MA 01341
413-369-4057
(fax) 413-369-4299
www.southrivermiso.com
Organic miso products

SPECTRUM ORGANIC, INC.

1304 South Point Blvd., Suite 280
Petaluma, CA 94954
707-778-8900
(fax) 707-765-8470
www.spectrumorganic.com
Spectrum Spread and oils

TIMBER CREST FARMS

4791 Dry Creek Rd.
Healdsburg, CA 95448
888-374-9325
707-433-8251
(fax) 707-433-8255
tcf@timbercrest.com
*Nonsulfured organic sun-dried fruits and
vegetables*

TUMARO'S GOURMET TORTILLAS

5300 Santa Monica Blvd., Suite 311
Los Angeles, CA 90029
323-464-6317
www.tumaros.com
Tortillas and snacks

WHOLE FOODS

www.wholefoods.com
Large retailer of natural and organic foods

WILDOATS MARKETS

800-494-WILD
www.wildoats.com
Large retailer of natural and organic foods

INDEX

CONVERSION CHART

American cooks use standard containers, the 8-ounce cup and a tablespoon that takes exactly 16 level fillings to fill that cup level. Measuring by cup makes it very difficult to give weight equivalents, as a cup of densely packed butter will weigh considerably more than a cup of flour. The easiest way therefore to deal with cup measurements in recipes is to take the amount by volume rather than by weight. Thus the equation reads:

1 cup = 240 ml = 8 fl. oz.   ½ cup = 120 ml = 4 fl. oz.

It is possible to buy a set of American cup measures in major stores around the world.

In the States, butter is often measured in sticks. One stick is the equivalent of 8 tablespoons. One tablespoon of butter is therefore the equivalent to ½ ounce/15 grams.

LIQUID MEASURES

Fluid Ounces	U.S.	Imperial	Milliliters
	1 teaspoon	1 teaspoon	5
¼	2 teaspoons	1 dessertspoon	10
½	1 tablespoon	1 tablespoon	14
1	2 tablespoons	2 tablespoons	28
2	¼ cup	4 tablespoons	56
4	½ cup		110
5		¼ pint or 1 gill	140
6	¾ cup		170
8	1 cup		225
9			250, ¼ liter
10	1¼ cups	½ pint	280
12	1½ cups		340
15		¾ pint	420
16	2 cups		450
18	2¼ cups		500, ½ liter
20	2½ cups	1 pint	560
24	3 cups		675
25		1¼ pints	700
27	3½ cups		750
30	3¾ cups	1½ pints	840
32	4 cups or 1 quart		900
35		1¾ pints	980
36	4½ cups		1000, 1 liter
40	5 cups	2 pints or 1 quart	1120

SOLID MEASURES

U.S. and Imperial Measures		Metric Measures	
Ounces	Pounds	Grams	Kilos
1		28	
2		56	
3½		100	
4	¼	112	
5		140	
6		168	
8	½	225	
9		250	¼
12	¾	340	
16	1	450	
18		500	½
20	1¼	560	
24	1½	675	
27		750	¾
28	1¾	780	
32	2	900	
36	2¼	1000	1
40	2½	1100	
48	3	1350	
54		1500	1½

OVEN TEMPERATURE EQUIVALENTS

Fahrenheit	Celsius	Gas Mark	Description
225	110	¼	Cool
250	130	½	
275	140	1	Very Slow
300	150	2	
325	170	3	Slow
350	180	4	Moderate
375	190	5	
400	200	6	Moderately Hot
425	220	7	Fairly Hot
450	230	8	Hot
475	240	9	Very Hot
500	250	10	Extremely Hot

Any broiling recipes can be used with the grill of the oven, but beware of high-temperature grills.

EQUIVALENTS FOR INGREDIENTS

all-purpose flour—plain flour
baking sheet—oven tray
cheesecloth—muslin
coarse salt—kitchen salt
cornstarch—cornflour

eggplant—aubergine
granulated sugar—caster sugar
parchment paper—greaseproof paper
plastic wrap—cling film

scallion—spring onion
zest—rind
zucchini—courgettes or marrow